PUB WA
IN
Cheshire

James F. Edwards

COUNTRYSIDE BOOKS
NEWBURY BERKSHIRE

First published 1994
© James F. Edwards 1994
Reprinted 1996, 1998, 2000, 2004
New Edition 2007

COUNTRYSIDE BOOKS
3 Catherine Road
Newbury, Berkshire

To view our complete range of books,
please visit us at
www.countrysidebooks.co.uk

ISBN 978 1 84674 045 9

*This book is dedicated
to the members of
The Thursday Group, Wilmslow,
whose activities usually focus upon a pub!*

The cover picture shows the locks on the
Peak Forest canal at Marple and was supplied by
Pictures of Britain (Lachlan Main)

Photographs by the author

Designed by Peter Davies, Nautilus Design
Produced through MRM Associates Ltd., Reading
Typeset by CJWT Solutions, St Helens
Printed by Information Press, Oxford

Contents

AREA MAP SHOWING LOCATION OF THE WALKS

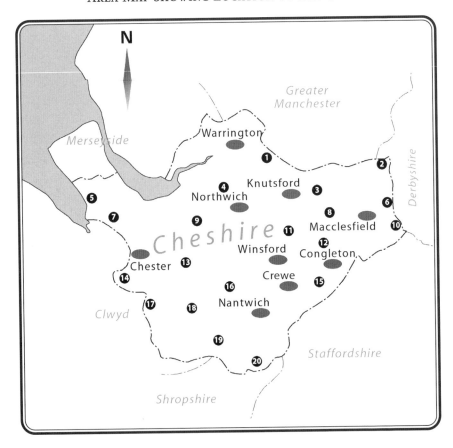

Walk

PUBLISHER'S NOTE

We hope that you obtain considerable enjoyment from this book; great care has been taken in its preparation. However, changes of landlord and actual closures are sadly not uncommon. Likewise, although at the time of publication all routes followed public rights of way or permitted paths, diversion orders can be made and permissions withdrawn.

We cannot of course be held responsible for such diversion orders and any inaccuracies in the text which result from these or any other changes to the routes, nor any damage which might result from walkers trespassing on private property. However, we are anxious that all details covering the walks and the pubs are kept up to date and would therefore welcome information from readers which would be relevant to future editions.

The simple sketch maps that accompany the walks in this book are based on notes made by the author whilst checking out the routes on the ground. However, for the benefit of a proper map, we do recommend that you purchase the relevant Ordnance Survey sheet covering your walk. The Ordnance Survey maps are widely available, especially through booksellers and local newsagents.

INTRODUCTION

Having now completed a number of walking guides relating to the county of Cheshire, I am still surprised by the diversity of scenery contained within such a small geographical area. However, no amount of descriptive prose can act as a substitute, or adequately compensate, for actually observing this scenery at first-hand. Thus this guide has been written, not to provide light reading, but to be used out in the field to escort the user along the footpaths, highways and byways of rural Cheshire.

The walks have been designed to give a taste of the variety of the Cheshire countryside, whilst at the same time enabling the participants to enjoy the atmosphere and offerings of some of the finest inns in the county.

Partake in a seaside walk on the Wirral Peninsula; meander amongst the hills of the Peak District National Park; walk beside river, mere and canal; stroll across the rich farming country of the central Cheshire Plain and gaze upon characterful black and white dwellings; all this, and a host of idyllic picturesque villages and centuries-old churches just waiting to be explored.

As well as varied scenery, Cheshire can also boast a tremendous variety of inns, making the task of selection a difficult one. The inns at the centre of each walk all have their own innate character and range from the unpretentious but warm, welcoming houses in the hills, to the more sophisticated hostelries found in the villages of the Cheshire Plain.

For centuries the inn has been an intrinsic part of Cheshire life with many of the older establishments having started out as farms which gradually developed into licensed premises. The landlords of these forerunners of present-day Cheshire inns would be amazed at the range of drink and food taken for granted by the modern traveller.

It should be noted that specific opening times have not been included in the individual pub descriptions – due to the fact that they are constantly changing. However, these can always be obtained by using the telephone number which is given at the end of each description. Also, where the menu is the subject of constant change, only an outline of the type of food available is given. Again, each individual pub can be contacted in order to obtain specific menu details.

Furthermore, it must be stressed that parking is only for patrons. Alternative parking locations, when available, have been indicated in the text.

Footwear is important. Waterproof walking shoes or boots are recommended, preferably worn over woollen socks. Smooth-soled shoes should not be worn as they can cause accidents and make walking hard work, especially after wet weather. Lightweight waterproof clothing should always be carried to combat the variable English weather. A small rucksack can be useful for carrying such items as food, cameras, binoculars and the like, which help to make a walk that much more enjoyable.

A prime objective has been to provide direct, no-nonsense route details for each walk, coupled with a clear accompanying sketch map. For those requiring more detail, the relevant OS Landranger 1:50 000 map numbers are given.

Do not be afraid to venture out during the winter months, for an excursion on a cold clear day when the frost has hardened the ground underfoot can be most rewarding, especially when coupled with a warming drink and a hearty meal taken in pleasant surroundings. However, if you wish to enjoy the facilities of an inn following the completion of a walk please remember to leave muddy walking boots in your car.

Finally, some words of thanks. Although my mother did not accompany me during the survey for this particular book, she did make a valued contribution to the finished work. I must also thank all the managers and landlords of the various inns for taking time from their busy schedules in order to answer my many questions.

James F. Edwards

1 LITTLE BOLLINGTON

The Swan With Two Nicks

THIS WALK WILL TAKE YOU THROUGH THE LOVELY ESTATE OF DUNHAM MASSEY WITH ITS MAGNIFICENT HALL, WHERE HERDS OF FALLOW DEER ROAM FREELY THROUGHOUT A GLORIOUS PARKLAND SETTING. THE ROUTE THEN CUTS ACROSS DUNHAM FOREST GOLF COURSE TO DUNHAM TOWN (ACTUALLY A VILLAGE) AND ALONG THE TOWPATH OF THE BRIDGEWATER CANAL BEFORE RETURNING TO LITTLE BOLLINGTON VIA FIELD PATHS, LANES AND TRACKS.

It is fortuitous that so many of our footpaths pass through the parklands of great estates, thus giving the walker a glimpse of an environment which is hundreds of years old.

LITTLE BOLLINGTON – *The Swan with Two Nicks*

THE SWAN WITH TWO NICKS is a very attractive pub in a beautiful setting, close to the Dunham Massey Estate near the rippling waters of the river Bollin. The pub's name refers to the 'nicking' of a swan's beak - a practice that at one time was carried out to determine ownership.

Built in the early 19th century, the inn's interior exudes olde-worlde charm, with low beams, horse brasses and antiques round every corner. During summertime when all the flowers are in bloom the exterior is awash with colour and during winter there are glowing real fires to take away the chill.

A wide range of ale is available including Marston's Pedigree, Boddingtons, Whitbread Castle Eden Ale and Flowers. Dry Blackthorn cider is also served. The pub has a fine reputation for its food, offering a wide choice at sensible prices every day at lunchtime and in the evening. Bar food is also served. When the weather is fine you can enjoy the beer garden, where children and well-behaved dogs are welcome.

✆ 0161 928 2914

How to get there: The A56 road connects Altrincham with Lymm and Warrington. About 3 miles from Altrincham there is a roadside hotel called the Stamford Arms. Drive down Park Lane which commences at the side of the Stamford Arms and after ¼ mile arrive at the Swan With Two Nicks.

Parking: There is a car park at the side and rear of the Swan With Two Nicks, which walkers patronising the inn can use. Alternatively, there is laneside parking available close by the pub.

Length of the walk: 4 miles. Map: OS Landranger 109 Manchester (GR 729870).

THE WALK

1. On leaving the inn turn left and after 80 metres go over a metal footbridge taking you across the river Bollin. A large building on the left has recently been converted into a number of dwellings.

A gap at the side of a facing gate takes you on to a fenced-in gravel path. Across the fields, straight ahead and to the left, can be seen the imposing buildings of Dunham Hall. A straight length of path leads to a ladder-stile giving access to the grounds of Dunham Estate. Walk forward along a macadam drive and pass to the right of the old mill where a water-wheel can be seen through a gap in the mill building. The drive takes you to the front entrance drive of Dunham Hall, which is open to the general public every day of the week except Thursdays and Fridays, 12 noon to 5 pm from April to October inclusive. The National Trust inherited the Dunham Estate on the death of Roger Grey, tenth Earl of Stamford, in 1976. Adjacent buildings in this vicinity have been converted into a restaurant, tea room and gift shop. The way forks immediately on passing the entrance drive to the

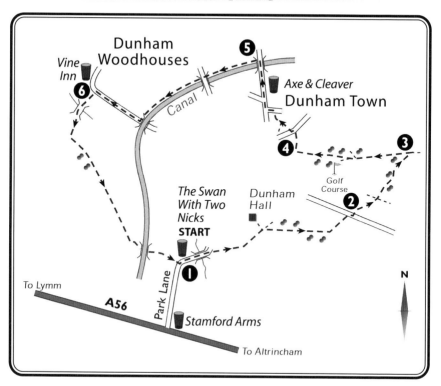

hall. Take the right fork here and follow a long, straight drive between trees. It is in this area that you are likely to see the fallow deer which roam freely throughout the estate. After a straight ½ mile follow the drive as it turns to the left. A ladder-stile close by a lodge house takes you out of the estate and on to a crossing road. Walk over the road, turn right, and then almost immediately turn left to pass through a gap in a wooden fence.

2 Follow a well-defined path through trees and undergrowth to arrive at a fairway of the Dunham Forest Golf Club. Bear diagonally right here and walk straight across the fairway – after first ensuring that you will not interfere with a golf match – and, after 100 metres, arrive at a crossing track. Walk straight across the track – there are signs here asking that you keep to the footpath – and cross another fairway. A well-defined footpath meanders through trees. Pass a low brick wall and then go over a crossing track to arrive at a T-junction where the way is sharp left.

3 Follow a track across another fairway and pass a short row of conifer trees. There are low-lying buildings on the right. Bear left and shortly turn right to follow a straight section of track through trees where there is an old wood and wire fence on your immediate left. On emerging walk forward and, keeping in the same direction as before, cross two fairways of the golf course then pass to the left of a raised green. On crossing another fairway leave the golf course via a stile in a facing hedgerow to enter a large field. Turn right and follow a field edge, keeping a hedgerow on your immediate right. Pass through a kissing gate and continue along the next field edge where the path is now fenced-in. On reaching the end of the field go through a kissing gate and turn left to follow a lane.

4 After only 50 metres, leave the lane to the right and go over a stile, then along a narrow path between fields. Keep forward at a junction of paths. The path is hedged-in now and leads to School Lane, where the way is right. On the right now is

Dunham Town post office and store. Walk past the head of Back Lane and continue. Across the road, on your left, is St Mark's church, built in 1864. Continue past the Axe and Cleaver Inn and the village hall, originally a school built in 1759, to arrive at a bridge which takes you over the Bridgewater Canal.

5 Cross the bridge and then leave the lane to the left and descend onto the towpath of the canal. Follow the towpath away from the bridge. Pass under the next bridge and continue along the towpath. After a further ½ mile the canal narrows briefly where a bridge passes over a lane. Cross the bridge, then leave the towpath to the right and descend an embankment. Go over a stile and turn left to follow the roadside pavement. Shortly, pass dwellings and enter the hamlet of Dunham Woodhouses. Just before Yew Tree Farm, turn left to enter Meadow Lane. (If you are in need of refreshment, the Vine Inn is just a few short strides past Yew Tree Farm.)

6 Continue along Meadow Lane and pass cottages (1825) then go over the river Bollin via a bridge. Immediately after crossing the bridge go over a facing stile to enter a field and bear diagonally left to follow a path which passes close to a telegraph pole. A footbridge takes you over a tributary of the Bollin. Climb up a facing grassy bank and go over a stile close by a telegraph pole. Walk to the next telegraph pole and turn sharp left – there is a footpath sign here. After 60 metres go over a stile at the side of a field gate. Follow a field edge, keeping a hedgerow on your immediate right. Go over a stile at the field corner to enter a large field. Keep forward now, aiming just to the right of a large electricity pylon which can be seen across the field about 250 metres away. Go over a stile at the side of a field gate close to the pylon. Follow a track and soon pass over another stile at the side of a gate. A facing tunnel takes you under the Bridgewater Canal. The track becomes a cobbled way leading to a junction with a lane. Turn left now and walk back to the Swan With Two Nicks and the car.

The Romper Inn

BEFORE THE BOUNDARY CHANGES OF 1976, THE WHOLE OF THE WALK WOULD HAVE BEEN WITHIN CHESHIRE, NOW ONLY HALF OF THE ROUTE IS IN THIS COUNTY – THE OTHER HALF BEING IN GREATER MANCHESTER. FORTUNATELY, THE SCENERY IS JUST THE SAME AS IT ALWAYS WAS AND THIS WALK PROVIDES A PLATFORM FOR LONG VIEWS ACROSS TO THE HILLS OF THE HIGH PEAK. THE RETURN LEG TAKES IN A SECTION OF THE PEAK FOREST CANAL PRIOR TO CLIMBING BACK TO THE ROMPER INN ALONG A NARROW LANE.

The Peak Forest Canal, which connects the Ashton Canal at Dukinfield with Whaley Bridge, was constructed during the final decade of the 18th century – primarily for the transportation of limestone from the Buxton area of Derbyshire. Prior to this time, the site of the Romper Inn was occupied by a row of cottages. The thirsty work of canal building was recognised by the enterprising owners of these cottages with the result that the Romper Inn came into being.

THE ROMPER INN retains an olde-worlde atmosphere, and is well known for its range of beers, where thirst-quenchers such as Wadworth 6X and Theakston Old Peculier compete with the likes of Timothy Taylor Landlord and draught Dry Blackthorn cider. The inn also has an excellent reputation for its food, which is served every lunchtime and evening (on Sunday, food is served from 12 noon until 9.45 pm). The menu must be one of the most comprehensive of any similar establishment in the north-west. Virtually any type of meal can be purchased and the choice is constantly changing. Keep an eye open for the 'Specials Board' where additional delicacies are chalked up. The inn has a beer garden where children are welcome but the landlord asks that dogs are not taken into the building.

✆ 0161 427 1354

How to get there: The Romper Inn is situated in a somewhat remote place. There are two approaches. From Marple, drive along Church Lane, which commences at the junction of the A626 and A627 roads. Church Lane climbs and becomes Ridge Road which takes you over a hill and on to the Romper Inn. From High Lane, drive up Carr Brow, which joins the A6 road at a bend on the Disley side, and then turn left to enter Wybersley Road. One mile further along this twisty road brings you to the Romper Inn.

Parking: The Romper Inn has ample parking for patrons. Alternative parking is available at a car park a little further up the hill from the inn at Ridge Quarry Viewpoint.

Length of the walk: 3 miles. Map: OS Landranger 109 Manchester (GR 965866).

THE WALK

1 On leaving the inn pass Ridge End Fold and Ridge End Farm to descend along a roadside pavement. At the bottom of the descent, and opposite the entrance drive of Lea Cote Farm, leave

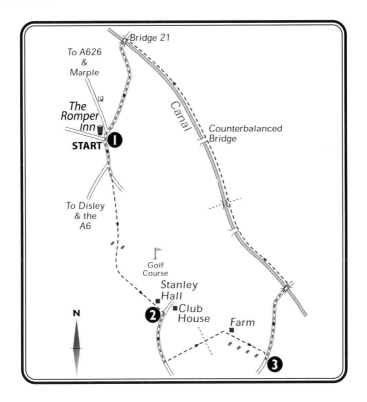

Wybersley Road and fork left to enter Turf Lea. After 80 metres, turn right and pass over a stone stile to enter a field. A straight path takes you to a stile which is located to the right of a row of houses. The route takes you past the end of the gardens belonging to the houses and over another stile. On passing over this stile follow a field edge, pass over another stile, then skirt to the right around a small pond. Bear left to the field corner and go over a stile, to continue along a field edge keeping a hedgerow on your immediate left. Shortly, there is a junction of paths. Pass through a kissing gate here and keep forward in the direction of Jackson's Edge. Walk across the corner of a field, then go through a gate in a crossing fence. There is an isolated stone chimney about 50 metres away on the left here. Descend and then climb to go over a stile at the side of a facing gate and ascend along a stony track through trees. Emerge from the trees and cross one of the fairways of Disley Golf Course. Walk forward to join a track. Keep to the left of a facing bank to follow the track which gradually climbs. The track turns to the left and continues across the golf course where there are long views to the distant hills of the Peak National Park.

2 After you pass Stanley Hall, (which, alas, has seen better days), there is a junction of ways. Down to the left is the large club house belonging to the golf course, but turn right here to gradually ascend along a macadam drive. On the left shortly is an interesting wooden shelter topped by a weather-vane. As you emerge from Disley Golf Course turn left through a gate and follow a fenced-in track which descends towards Stanley Hall Farm. The track leads to a gate which gives access to a farm, but turn right and leave the track about 20 metres before the gate to pass through a gate in a hedge. Cross a narrow field keeping the farm outbuildings about 30 metres away to your left. Go over a stile in a crossing fence and descend along the right-hand edge of a large sloping field. There are long views to the facing hills from this section of the path. Cross a stile at the base of a very large tree to emerge on to a narrow lane.

3 Turn left, pass a dwelling, and ascend the lane. Pass the entrance drive of Haycroft, then descend to go over a counterbalanced bridge giving access to the towpath of the Peak Forest Canal. Turn left and walk beside the canal, an endless source of fascination with its boats and wildlife. Down on the right is the valley of the river Goyt where gaps through the trees offer glimpses of the village of Strines. Follow the towpath for 1 mile, passing under bridges 23 and 21 en route. At bridge 21 leave the towpath and walk over the bridge. Bear left and follow a narrow lane past the rear of a couple of dwellings fronting the canal. The lane climbs past a number of dwellings and takes you back to the Romper Inn and the car.

The Bull's Head and Roebuck Inns

THE WALK HEADS AWAY FROM THE VILLAGE ALONG LANES, TRACKS AND CROSS-COUNTRY PATHS, THEN THROUGH THE PARISH OF GREAT WARFORD BEFORE RETURNING ALONG A DELIGHTFUL PATH WHICH NEVER STRAYS TOO FAR FROM THE BUBBLING WATERS OF MOBBERLEY BROOK.

Mobberley can boast of a long history, going back centuries before its mention in the Domesday Book. The village possesses many attractive and interesting buildings of varied styles which are a delight to the discerning visitor. It can also boast two superb inns, both dating back to the 17th century and only metres apart at the start of a splendid walk! It would have been unfair to leave one out, therefore both have been included.

THE BULL'S HEAD has open coal fires, a wealth of oak beams, its own bowling green and a beer garden. Inside, the walls are adorned with photographs of old Mobberley. The inn provides traditional hand-pulled ales from Tetley, Boddingtons and Jennings of Cumbria. Draught Strongbow cider is also available. There is a range of real home-cooked lunches at very reasonable prices and, for snacks, you can choose from a wide range of traditional and toasted sandwiches.
✆ 01565 873134

THE ROEBUCK has, during recent years, been internally modernised using floorboards recycled from a local mill and the seating is in the form of pews. There is an adjacent beer garden. The inn serves beers from Boddingtons, Ruddles, Courage and John Smith's together with Scrumpy and draught Strongbow cider. Food is available every lunchtime and evening. Two menus are always provided, one for full meals and the other for snacks. The choice includes several daily special dishes, and the range of food is excellent and varies with the season, each main course being complemented by locally grown produce.
✆ 01565 873322

How to get there: Mobberley straddles the B5085 between Knutsford and Wilmslow. The road dips through a hollow on the Wilmslow side of the village at the junction with Mill Lane. Drive along Mill Lane and after 150 metres arrive at the inns.
Parking: Both inns have car parks. Alternatively, park on Mill Lane, although space is somewhat limited.
Length of the walk: 3½ miles. Map: OS Landranger 118 Stoke-on-Trent and Macclesfield (GR 789796).

THE WALK

1 Enter Damson Lane which commences opposite the Bull's Head and runs along one side of the Roebuck car park. Climb along the lane past Damson Cottage where it becomes a grassy track.

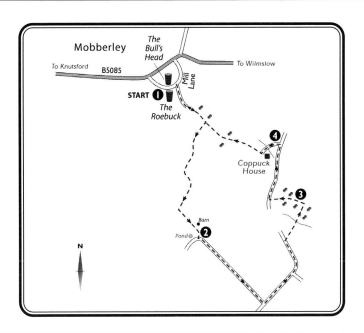

After 300 metres the track leads to a facing gate and metal kissing gate. Turn right and follow a path as it gradually climbs between hedges. Go through a wooden gate and continue. After 100 metres go through a metal gate at the side of a larger gate to enter a large field. Continue in the same general direction as before and follow the field edge, keeping trees and hedges on your immediate right.

Turn left at the end of the field, again keeping a hedge on your immediate right. After 80 metres arrive at the field corner and go through a metal gate to enter a large field. Across the field, about 400 metres away, a modern barn can be seen. Keep along the field edge with a hedgerow and trees on your immediate right. Turn left at the field corner and continue, still with a hedgerow on your right. Pass between the modern barn and the hedgerow on your right to arrive at a gate which gives access to a macadam drive. Turn left and walk along the drive.

2 A straight ½ mile leads to a crossing lane, where the way is left.

You are now walking along Pedley House Lane. A straight ¼ mile takes you past Ancoats Lane which goes off to the right. Enter Faulkner's Lane and follow this as it bends to the left. Continue to where a pavement begins on the left at a dwelling called The Headmasters House. Go over a stile opposite this dwelling to enter a large rough field. Follow the field edge keeping a hedgerow on your immediate left. At the field corner go over a footbridge which takes you across Mobberley Brook. There is a fence on the left side of the path now. About 150 metres after crossing the brook go over a stile on the left.

3 Walk to, and go over, a stile which can be seen about 60 metres away, straight ahead. Cross a plank-bridge and go over another stile to enter a narrow field. Climb forward up a grassy bank. Straight ahead there is a dwelling. Walk forward and keep to the left of the garden hedge to arrive at a stile at the side of a gate. Cross the stile to once again enter Faulkner's Lane, where the way is right. Gradually climb and pass the ornate entrance gate of Antrobus Hall.

4 After a further 250 metres turn left to enter a macadam drive commencing at the side of a house called Merrydale. There is a footpath sign here and a sign indicating Coppuck House. Follow the drive over Mobberley Brook and pass through a gateway topped by a pair of stone lions. Turn immediately right and cross a concreted area to go over a stile at the right-hand side of a field gate. Follow a field edge, keeping a hedgerow on your immediate right. At the field corner go over another stile and continue, again with a hedgerow on your immediate right. At the next field corner, which is sometimes boggy, go over a stile and climb up a bank to enter a large undulating field. Cross the field, bearing right, to arrive at a metal kissing gate by a facing gate. Go through the kissing gate and walk forward along a track. You are now back on part of the route you took earlier in the walk. The track leads back to Damson Lane which in turn takes you back to the inn and the car.

The Chetwode Arms

THE FIRST HALF OF THE WALK IS ALONG FIELD PATHS AND OVER STILES FOLLOWED BY A GENTLE MILE ALONG A NARROW, HALF-FORGOTTEN, RURAL LANE ON THE APPROACHES TO HIGHER WHITLEY. A SHORT STROLL AROUND THE VILLAGE PRECEDES THE RETURN TO LOWER WHITLEY.

There are two Whitleys, once variously known as Over and Nether Whitley or Whitley Superior and Inferior. Now the names have settled into Higher and Lower Whitley. Today's jaunt provides an opportunity to explore both places. The return journey is along a lane taking you between half-hidden pools where fishermen from near and far practise their skills.

THE CHETWODE ARMS is named after a family of local landowners. Much of the building which is today the Chetwode Arms is over 300 years old. The inn is very near St Luke's church

and this closeness was used to good effect when the old custom of 'roping' used to take place. After a wedding, the route of the happy couple was barred by a rope which was removed only on payment of the price of a good drink. This custom was carried out as recently as 1968. The inn has many rooms and two bars. The lounge, with its sloping floor, has french windows opening on to an attractive bowling green. Greenall Whitley beers are served including mild, bitter and hand-pulled original ale as well as draught Strongbow cider. The Chetwode Arms is well known for its fine food, served at lunchtime and in the evening. If the weather is fine refreshments may be taken at tables overlooking the immaculate bowling green. In cooler weather there are no fewer than five real fires to warm you.
ℰ 01925 730203

How to get there: Lower Whitley is just off the A49, 6 miles to the south of Warrington and 2 miles to the south of junction 10 of the M56. The Chetwode Arms is at the centre of the village not far from the church.

Parking: The inn has a large car park. Alternatively, there is a lay-by at the side of the A49 about 300 metres from Street Lane, which leads into the village of Lower Whitley.

Length of the walk: 3½ miles. Map: OS Landranger 118 Stoke-on-Trent and Macclesfield (GR 614789).

THE WALK

1 Enter a hedged-in footpath directly opposite the inn. Pass to the rear of the church grounds and leave the path over a stile. Keep forward, in the same direction as before, and pass close to the corner of a fence to a stile. Cut across the corner of a field and after 70 metres go over a stile at the side of a telegraph pole. Follow the edge of a large field, keeping a hedgerow on your immediate left. Go through a gate at the field corner and bear right to follow a farm approach track. After 60 metres go through a facing gate and turn left just before the farmyard to

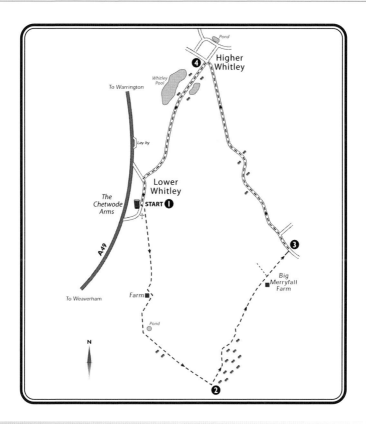

go over a stile at the side of another gate. Keep close by the farm garden hedgerow and follow it to the right after about 20 metres. A straight 80 metres leads to a stile in a crossing hedgerow. Go over the stile, then bear left to pass to the right of a fenced-in pond half overgrown with bullrushes. On passing the pond bear left to go over a stile in a facing fence to the left of a small copse. Continue, keeping a fence on your immediate right, to walk along the edge of a large field. About 30 metres before the field corner is reached go over a stile in the fence on your right and continue in the same direction as before with the fence, and then a hedgerow, on your left.

2 As you approach a large wood go over a fence-stile and pass

through trees and undergrowth and then go over a stile on the left to proceed along a field edge, keeping trees on your right. There is a pond among the trees on your right. The path meanders around the edge of the wood. Where the trees finish there are two brick and concrete manhole structures about 6 ft square. From this point the way is along a track which gradually climbs towards buildings. The track follows a field edge where there is a hedgerow on the left which takes you to the left of Big Merryfall Farm. Pass a track going off to the left and follow a straight stretch taking you to a crossing lane.

3 Turn left along the lane which shortly turns sharply to the right, but keep forward here to enter Back Lane. On passing a three-storey dwelling, built in 1741, the lane becomes a hedged-in track. Emerge at a facing gate and follow the track along a field edge. Pass through another gate and continue past a couple of dwellings on the left. The track has given way to a narrow winding macadam lane taking you to a crossroads on the edge of the village of Higher Whitley.

4 The route back to Lower Whitley is along Village Lane off to the left, but first turn to the right and take a look at the village of Higher Whitley. The village has retained an old-fashioned atmosphere and has many interesting buildings. On turning next left there is a delightful scene across a large pond which is the home of many species of water fowl. Turn next left and pass the head of Dark Lane. On turning left again you will arrive back at the crossroads opposite Back Lane.

Turn right now to proceed along Village Lane. Pass the school and shortly arrive at a walled-in area on the right. This is a Quaker burial ground where the oldest recorded burial relates to John Starkey (1657). At the rear of the burial ground you will see the deep waters of Whitley Pool. Village Lane leads to the outskirts of Lower Whitley where the way is left in the direction of Dones Green and past Village Farm. A few more strides and you are back at the Chetwode Arms.

5 PARKGATE

The Boat House

THIS WALK HAS A DISTINCT SEASIDE FLAVOUR, WITH THE DELIGHTFUL OLD PORT OF PARKGATE HAVING MANY APPEALING HOUSES AND FISHERMEN'S COTTAGES. THE LONG PROMENADE HAS OLD-FASHIONED SHOPS SELLING FRESH SEAFOOD AND HOME MADE ICE-CREAM. THE WALK, WHICH IS FLAT AND EASY GOING, TAKES YOU OUT TO THE NORTH OF THE TOWN WHERE A FOOTPATH FOLLOWS THE SEA WALL. THE ROUTE THEN CUTS INLAND ALONG A LANE TO JOIN THE WIRRAL WAY FOR THE RETURN JOURNEY TO PARKGATE.

Parkgate was a bustling port during the 18th and early 19th centuries, with ships regularly sailing to Ireland. Today it is hard to imagine deep water lapping against the sea wall, although an occasional high tide gives some impression of how things must have appeared then. When the roads to Holyhead were improved, the journey by sea to Ireland was halved, and the fortunes of Parkgate declined. The ensuing silting of the Dee estuary ended the village's role as a port.

THE BOAT HOUSE is situated at the end of The Parade, and has an attractive black and white exterior. There has been an inn on this site for many long years and the building must have presented a welcoming site to sailors of yesteryear approaching Parkgate in rough weather. The inn has recently been renovated and has a characterful interior where meals and drinks can be taken in comfort whilst looking out across the Dee Estuary towards Wales. A comprehensive range of refreshment is available, and food is served between 12 noon and 9.30 pm (Sunday 6 pm and closed on Monday). Children are welcome inside until 7 pm.

℘ 0151 3364187

How to get there: The A540 connects Chester with Hoylake on the Wirral peninsula. Approximately midway the secondary B5134 runs in a westerly direction from the A540 and, after 1 mile, passes through Neston; then it is a further mile to Parkgate. The Boat House is at the end of The Parade, a long promenade looking out across the Dee Estuary.

Parking: The inn has a large car park.

Length of the walk: 4½ miles. Map: OS Landranger 117 Chester and 108 Liverpool (GR 279782).

THE WALK

(1) On leaving the inn, turn left and walk past a sign indicating Wirral Country Park. Follow a roadside pavement and pass a large detached dwelling on the right called The Bath House. The way leads to a parking area for vehicles at the end of which there is a junction of footpaths. A sign to the right points towards the Wirral Way, but keep forward here to go through a facing gap. Follow a path which hugs the shoreline and follows the course of the sea wall. This area is a favourite location for bird-

watchers who come with their binoculars and telescopes to observe the various species.

Shortly, over to the right, there is a golf course and a little further on the footpath actually runs along the top of the sea wall. Eventually, the path takes you, via steps, to a lane.

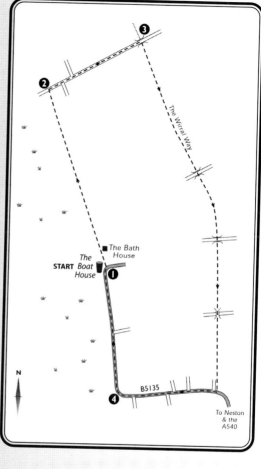

2 Follow the lane and pass Cottage Drives East and West. The lane gradually climbs now, with tall hedgerows on both sides, then passes over a bridge.

3 Leave the lane to the right after a further 30 metres, through a gap by a gate. Descend to a footpath created from the defunct Neston to Hoylake railway line. Turn left, and walk away from the bridge you have just crossed; that is, in the direction of Neston. Follow a clearly defined tree-lined path that cuts across the golf course you glimpsed earlier in the walk. You are on the Wirral Way, part of a linear park which has been created for the enjoyment of walkers. There are a number of strategically positioned seats along the way where you can rest and enjoy the views across the Dee Estuary.

Almost 1 mile after joining the Wirral Way, pass under Backwood Hall Bridge and continue along the footpath. After a further 500 metres, pass under Boathouse Lane Bridge, and a little over ¼ mile further on, pass over a bridge which takes the footpath over a lane. The path is elevated in this area and quite heavily wooded on both sides and takes you to facing undergrowth. Turn right and then left to follow a cobbled way which in the days of the railway, was an approach to Parkgate Station. Emerge on to The Ropewalk, turn left, and after 30 metres arrive at a crossing-road. Turn right and walk along the roadside pavement. Pass Neston Cricket Club and the head of Grenfell Park.

Shortly on the right, and opposite the Old Quay Hotel, there is a row of cottages. The end cottage (No 16) is said to be the place where the then Emily Lyon stayed in June 1784 when she came to Parkgate to take the waters in an attempt to cure a skin complaint. Later she became Lady Emma Hamilton and subsequently the mistress of Lord Nelson.

④ Turn right on passing the cottages and walk along The Parade. The large black and white building on the right is Mostyn House School. During the 18th century this building was an inn and records tell us that the great German composer George Frederick Handel stayed here. The noted medical missionary, Sir Wilfred Thomason Grenfell, was born at Mostyn House in 1865. He went on to establish hospitals, missions and homes in Labrador and Newfoundland and was knighted in 1927. A little further along The Parade is one of Parkgate's well-known home-made ice-cream shops. The wide expanse of the Dee Estuary on your left reaches across to the shores of Wales and, if the day is clear, you should be able to make out the dark shape of Flint Castle, 7 miles away. On reaching the end of The Parade, arrive back at the Boat House inn and the car.

The Robin Hood Inn

THERE CAN BE NO DOUBT ABOUT THE MAIN ATTRACTION OF THIS WALK – THE MAGNIFICENT VIEWS OVER THE CHESHIRE PLAIN AND THE HILLS OF THE PEAK NATIONAL PARK SEEN FROM A PATH WHICH TRAVERSES THE BACKBONE OF KERRIDGE HILL. THE WALK RETURNS TO RAINOW VIA FIELD PATHS, TRACKS AND LANES.

◆●◆

The unusual edifice of White Nancy is a place to tarry whilst taking in a view over Bollington where many of the stone buildings remind us of the industries of the 18th and 19th centuries. The area has long been associated with quarrying and the local stone is considered to be of excellent quality; indeed, the cathedral at Coventry is paved with Kerridge stone.

THE ROBIN HOOD INN has stood above the scattered village of Rainow for many years and was previously known as the Robin Hood and Little John. By 1834 Little John appears to have fallen out of favour for, after that date, the inn has been recorded simply as the Robin Hood. Exactly where the connection with Robin Hood comes from is unknown. The inn is an unpretentious homely place where draught cider, a range of Greenalls Whitley beers and a good choice of inexpensive meals can be consumed in a warm and friendly atmosphere. Meals are served daily at lunchtime and in the evenings. If the weather happens to be on the chilly side the landlord ensures that his guests have the benefit of roaring log fires in the bar, dining area and family room. There is also an outdoor beer garden where customers may eat their own food when meals are not available, assuming that drinks are bought of course.

✆ 01625 574060

How to get there: Rainow lies on the A5002, 3 miles to the north-east of Macclesfield. The Robin Hood Inn fronts on to this road on the north side of the village.

Parking: There is a large car park for patrons at the side of the inn, and alternative limited laneside parking in Smithy Lane, which commences at the side of the inn.

Length of the walk: 3½ miles. Map: OS Landranger 118 Stoke-on-Trent and Macclesfield (GR 953762).

THE WALK

1 On leaving the Robin Hood Inn enter Stocks Lane which commences almost opposite the entrance to the car park. This lane takes its name from the location of the village stocks which sit on a bank close to the head of the lane. Follow the lane as it descends past Chapel Lane to join the Macclesfield road. Cross here and follow the roadside pavement descending past the church. At the bottom cross over the infant river Dean and then climb past the war memorial. The roadside pavement reaches more level terrain.

2 Opposite the end of the roadside pavement is the start of a

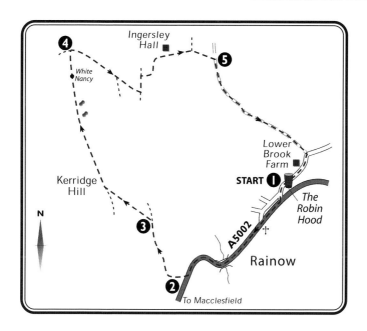

footpath where a sign informs you that you are on the 'Gritstone Trail'. Follow a track between stone walls. At a junction of paths, keep forward through a facing gateway between stone pillars and follow a well-defined path through scattered trees. Emerge from the trees through a gate set in a stone wall and continue with a stone wall and hawthorn trees on your immediate left. After 100 metres go over a fence-stile at the side of a gate close by a holly bush. Immediately on crossing this the path forks.

3 There is a level grassy track straight ahead but take a deep breath and climb the left-hand path to the side of Kerridge Hill. The path leads to a stile in a crossing stone wall. Rest for a minute or two here and admire the view over Rainow and to the hills beyond. Continue up the hillside (the going is easier now) and emerge on the backbone ridge of Kerridge Hill via a stile. Turn right and proceed along a ridge-top path which hugs a wall on the right. The views are quite superb. Pass through a couple of gates, and arrive at White Nancy. This edifice resembles a whitewashed sugar loaf and was built in memory of the Battle of Waterloo. Until recently it was possible to sit inside, but because of vandalism the entrance has now been blocked up. White Nancy looks straight out over the town of Bollington where the silver threads of the Macclesfield Canal can be picked out as it winds past dwelling and mill. From White Nancy descend along a steep path which takes you down the facing hillside.

④ At a crossing drive turn right and pass shortly through a gate at the side of a cattle grid. Keep left and soon descend along a narrow lane, between walls at first, and then with a wall only on the right. Pass through a gate at the side of a cattle grid then turn left at the junction ahead to follow a drive. After 80 metres leave the track over a stile on the right which takes you into a field. Shortly pass over a small stone bridge then walk forward and bear left to climb along a grassy track taking you up the side of a bank. Pass through a kissing gate, ascend steps, then pass through another kissing gate to enter a field. Keep along the left side of the field where there is a wall on the immediate left. Pass through another couple of kissing gates and continue, keeping close to the stone wall on the left. On the other side of the wall is Ingersley Hall, once the home of the Gaskill family who were responsible for the construction of White Nancy.

Go through a kissing gate to enter a large field. Ignore a stone stile on the left here and keep forward in the same general direction as before, gradually bearing right to diverge away from a stone wall on your left. Go through a gate to enter a walled-in track.

⑤ Turn right and proceed along the track. Shortly, Rainow comes into view over to the right. The track emerges on to a lane where the way is right to pass the three-storey farmhouse of Lower Brook Farm, The lane takes you back to the Robin Hood Inn and the car.

The Yacht Inn

THIS EASY WALK OVER THE FLAT AGRICULTURAL LANDS OF THE SOUTH WIRRAL PRESENTS AN IDEAL OPPORTUNITY TO GET AWAY FROM IT ALL. IT IS A WALK WHERE YOUR STILE-CLIMBING ABILITIES WILL BE TESTED TO THE FULL, FOR THERE ARE 21 ASSORTED DEVICES TO TACKLE BEFORE COMPLETING THE JOURNEY BACK TO THE INN. MOST OF THE ROUTE IS ALONG QUIET FIELD PATHS WHICH PROVIDE A PERFECT PLATFORM FOR OBSERVING THE LOCAL WILDLIFE AT CLOSE QUARTERS.

The lane at the side of the Yacht Inn goes to Shotwick, just over 1 mile away. For centuries, before the river Dee silted up, Shotwick was a port. During those far-off days, the Yacht Inn was a favourite with local sailors who would walk from Shotwick to quench their thirsts.

THE YACHT INN offers an extremely wide choice of food and drink which can be consumed in a very attractively decorated setting and where large bay windows provide a bright ambience. Greenalls Local Bitter and Original Bitter are amongst the choices of beer, together with Strongbow and Scrumpy Jack ciders. The inn is a Millers Kitchen, resulting in a comprehensive choice of meals to suit every taste, served every day at lunchtime and during the evening. On Sundays a very reasonably priced traditional roast lunch is offered. The inn has a beer garden and a play area for children.
    ✆ 01244 880216

How to get there: The A540 connects Chester with Hoylake on the Wirral peninsula. Four miles from Chester, and close to where the M56 currently terminates, the A540 cuts across the A5117. The Yacht Inn fronts on to the A540, 1 mile from this intersection in the direction of Hoylake.
Parking: The inn has a large car park. Alternatively, there are a couple of lay-bys in the vicinity.
Length of the walk: 3½ miles. Map: OS Landranger 117 Chester (GR 355731).

THE WALK

1 From the inn, cross the main road, and turn right to follow the pavement. Pass the Old Post Office and 60 metres further on go over a stile on the left at the side of a gate. After 20 metres, pass over a stile at the side of a gateway to enter a large field. Walk forward now, keeping a hedgerow on the right about 30 metres away, to a stile visible at the side of a large tree across the field. Go over the stile, cross a short squat concrete plank-bridge and almost immediately cross another stile. Follow a footpath along

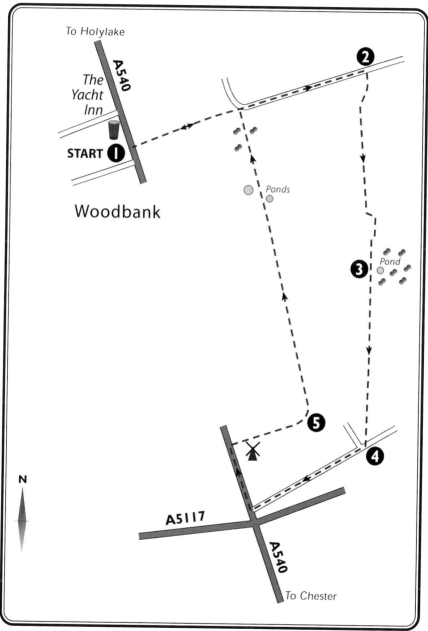

To Holylake

A540

The
Yacht
Inn

START ❶

Woodbank

❷

Ponds

❸ Pond

❺

N

❹

A5117

A540

To Chester

the left-hand edge of the next field, keeping a hedgerow, which is interspersed with trees, on your immediate left. Cross a stile at the field corner and emerge at a bend in a crossing lane. There is a footpath which goes off down a track on the right here but ignore this and walk forward along the lane. After 150 metres pass School House Farm. A little further on there is a row of cottages on the left and Keepers Cottage on the right.

2 Immediately on passing Keepers Cottage, leave the lane to the right, and go over a plank-bridge and stile by the cottage garden hedgerow to enter a large field. Walk along the right-hand edge of the field, with a hedgerow on your immediate right. Keep by the hedgerow as it turns slightly to the right. At the field corner go over a stile at the side of a gate. Continue along the next field edge, still with a hedgerow on your immediate right. On reaching the field corner, go over a stile at the side of a gate. As before, follow the right-hand edge of the next field. At the field corner turn left at the facing hedge, and after 20 metres go over a stile on the right at the side of a gate. You have now entered a field of coarse grass at the far side of which can be seen a wood. Follow the hedgerow on the right as it kinks to the right and left, then go over a stile in a crossing fence.

3 You have now entered a wooded area. The main wood, Big Wood, is over to your left. This area abounds with all manner of wildlife where time can be spent observing the birds, squirrels and other creatures in their natural habitat. Follow the facing path through the trees, in the same general direction as before. Pass a pond, and cross a stile at the side of a gate and leave the trees behind. Follow a track now, which stays close to a hedge, interspersed with trees, on the immediate right. Go over a stile at the side of a gate set in a crossing barbed-wire fence. Continue along the track and then go over a stile at the right-hand side of a gate. The track takes you in the general direction of a dwelling seen at the end of the field straight ahead. A stile at the field corner gives access to a path which takes you to the right of the dwelling and its garden shed. Arrive at a crossing lane, where the way is right.

4 Pass The Paddocks, a lane which goes off to the right. A straight ¼ mile along the lane takes you to the Chester to Hoylake road. Turn right here and follow the roadside pavement. After ¼ mile, arrive at the entrance drive of the Gibbet Windmill, a well-known landmark to travellers journeying to the Wirral. Immediately on passing the entrance drive, go over a stile on the right at the side of a field gate to enter a field. Walk forward, and after only 40 metres go over a stile and then 80 metres further on, pass over another stile and turn right to immediately pass over yet another stile at the side of a field gate.

5 Turn left and walk along the edge of another large field with the hedgerow on your immediate left. Go over a stile and plank-bridge at the field corner. Bear left now and pass a rough concrete stump to converge with a track near a field gate. Follow the track, which has an embankment on the left and a hedgerow interspersed with trees on the right. Where the embankment finishes, keep forward along the track and shortly pass ponds. A little further on, go over a stile at the side of a gate. The track is hedged-in now and emerges at a bend in a crossing lane. Go over a stile on the left here to follow the right-hand edge of a field. You are now back on part of the initial route. Follow the facing path, which leads back to the Chester to Hoylake road where you turn right for the short stroll back to the Yacht Inn.

Ye Olde Park Gate Inn

This walk is over level terrain and is easy going, making for an enjoyable evening stroll during the summer months when the days are long.

❖ ●● ❖

The name 'Peover' derives from the Anglo-Saxon 'Peeffer' – bright river. Unlike its counterpart, Lower Peover, Over Peover has no distinct village centre and is scattered over a wide area. During the Second World War, General George Patton lived for a time at Peover Hall and this walk will convey an impression of a tract of countryside that was so attractive to its founders.

OVER PEOVER – *Ye Olde Park Gate Inn*

YE OLDE PARK GATE INN was built over 200 years ago, and has remained predominantly unchanged. It was once a cobbler's shop and contains a large collection of old ladder-back Macclesfield chairs. Most of the beams are original and there are rustic brick fireplaces in every room. In the days when the inn provided refreshment for passing coach parties (the horse-drawn variety!) the landlord's wife would 'barbecue' meat on spits over the open fires. The liquid refreshment is provided by Yorkshire's oldest brewery – Samuel Smith – famed for providing beer from the wood to the majority of its pubs. Draught cider is also available. The inn has built up an excellent reputation for its food and there is a wide selection to choose from. Meals are served every lunchtime and evening. At the side of the inn there is an attractive garden with wooden tables and benches where children and well-behaved dogs are welcome.

Ø 01625 861455

How to get there: Much of the scattered village of Over Peover lies between the A50 and A537 3 miles to the south-east of Knutsford. About 2½ miles to the south of Knutsford there is a sharp bend in the A50 close to the Whipping Stocks Inn. Leave the A50 at this point, drive past the inn, and continue for just over 1 mile to arrive at Ye Olde Park Gate Inn.
Parking: There is a car park at the side of the inn.
Length of the walk: 3½ miles. Map: OS Landranger 118 Stoke-on-Trent and Macclesfield (GR 785739).

THE WALK

1) On leaving the inn, turn right and follow the roadside footpath past Mainwaring Road. Sixty metres after the path finishes, and immediately on passing the entrance drive of Colshaw Hall, turn right to enter a signed bridleway. The track is enclosed by a wooden fence on the right and hedgerow on the left. After about 300 metres, leave the track to the left over a stile, where

a footpath sign points across an extremely large field. A straight path of 250 metres takes you past a telegraph pole and leads to a farm approach drive.

2 Turn right now and follow the drive away from the farm. After 100 metres, the drive takes you over a deep dyke. After a further 100 metres there is a junction of ways. The way to the left goes to a farm, but keep right here and follow the drive to shortly pass through a gateway. On the right here is Lower Moss Wood, which is being developed as a nature reserve. The lane takes you past an isolated black and white cottage and then past Lower Mosswood House. A little further on, pass between a couple of facing dwellings – one of which is Ivy Old Cottage, and then 60

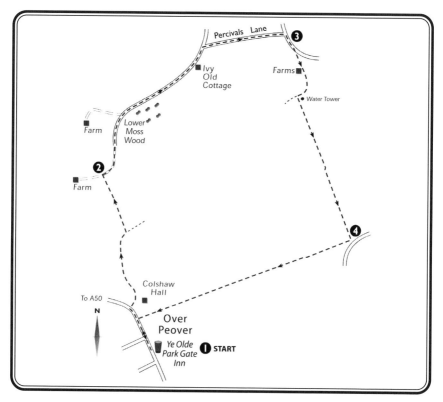

metres further on turn right to enter Percivals Lane. A straight
¼ mile leads to a T-junction, where the way is right.

3 After 80 metres leave the lane to the right and pass through a
gate to follow a track. A bridleway sign here points along the
track, which follows the edge of a field. Keep on past the
entrance to Bowden View Farm. The track is hedged-in now and
takes you past Oakwood Barn, The Old Farmhouse and The
Mouse House. On passing the entrance to Bowden Bank Farm,
go through a gateway and follow the track as it turns to the right
(there is a fence and also ponds on the immediate right here). On
the left now is a tall, concrete water tower, a dominant landmark.
Where the fencing enclosing the water tower finishes on the left
there is a stile. Cross this, then quickly cross a second stile and
continue forward along the edge of a large field with a fence,
hedge, and trees on your immediate right. At the field corner,
go over a stile on the right and continue in the same direction as
before with the fence, hedge and trees now on your immediate
left. There is a large dwelling straight ahead to the right. Keep
to the left of outbuildings and then pass through a gate.

4 Turn right 20 metres before arriving at a crossing lane and go
through a small gate to follow a narrow, hedged-in, path. A
straight 100 metres leads to a stile (the large dwelling previously
seen across the fields is on the immediate right here). On
crossing the stile keep forward to follow a field edge. At the field
corner go over another stile to enter open country. The path is
in the same direction as before and follows the line of large
widely spaced trees. The route takes you over a drive which goes
to a large red brick dwelling which can be seen over to the right.
Keep straight ahead in the same direction as before with a fence
now on your immediate left. There are many newly planted trees
in the vicinity. The path eventually leads to a stile at the side of
a field gate with dwellings on both sides. Cross the stile to
quickly arrive at a crossing road. Turn left now and follow the
roadside footpath back to Ye Olde Park Gate Inn.

The Carriers Inn

APART FROM OFFERING AN OPPORTUNITY TO RELAX BY THE WATERSIDE, THIS WALK PRESENTS A CHANCE TO EXPLORE THE COUNTRYSIDE AROUND DELAMERE FOREST. THERE IS A VISIT TO THE FOREST VILLAGE OF NORLEY AND THIS, COUPLED WITH A MIXTURE OF TRACKS, PATHS AND LANES, COMBINES TO OFFER A MOST REWARDING EXCURSION.

———◆◆———

Delamere Forest covers about 4,000 acres of rolling Cheshire countryside. One of the most attractive locations within the forest's boundaries is the lovely reed-fringed pool at Hatchmere.

THE CARRIERS INN enjoys an idyllic setting close by the still waters of Hatchmere lake, and has been in existence for over 300 years. Its name relates to the wagoners or carriers who used to stop here on their way to the port of Frodsham with agricultural produce, salt, cheese and other wares for loading onto sailing ships and barges. The inn is roomy, having a split-level lounge with highly varnished timbers presenting a pleasing appearance and where choices from the full range of Burtonwood ales can be consumed in comfort. Draught Woodpecker and Strongbow ciders are also available. Meals are served every day at lunchtime and during the evening. A 'Special Sunday Roast' extends the choice at weekends. The gardens at the rear of the inn lead down to Hatchmere lake. There is also a garden area where children can play.

✆ 01928 788258

How to get there: The B5152 connects Frodsham with the A556 near Delamere. About 4½ miles from Frodsham and 2½ miles from Delamere, is the attractive lakeside village of Hatchmere. The Carriers Inn fronts on to the B5152 only metres from the water's edge.

Parking: There is a car park at the side of the inn; alternatively a large public car park and picnic area are almost opposite the inn.

Length of the walk: 4½ miles. Map: OS Landranger 117 Chester (GR 554722).

THE WALK

1 On leaving the inn turn left, cross the road and enter a tree-lined track where a footpath sign points towards Norley Road and School Lane. After 120 metres, the track bends to the left, but walk forward here to follow a narrow path which is headed by a sign pointing to School Lane. The path leads through ferns and trees and emerges on to a gravel track. Keep forward along the track and then continue past another which goes off to the

left. Arrive at the junction of School Lane and Post Office Lane. Enter Post Office Lane and continue along the laneside pavement. Where the pavement peters out keep forward and gently descend along the lane.

② Leave the lane to the right now, just before a house on the right is reached, and enter a narrow hedged-in path which commences at the left-hand side of an electricity pole. After 100 metres pass through a gate and emerge into a sloping field. Keep to the right now, along the higher ground, with a tall unruly hedge on your

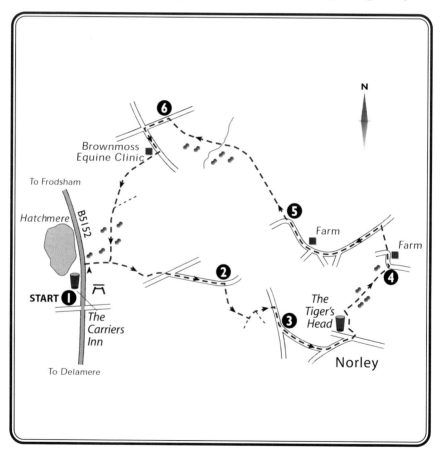

right. At the field corner, pass through a gate and turn left to follow a track. Pass close to dwellings, then keep forward, ignoring a track which goes off to the right. The facing track takes you to a crossing road. Go over the road and turn right to follow the roadside pavement.

3 On the right is Norley village hall, but turn left now to enter Maddocks Hill. On the immediate right at this point is Norley Central Methodist church. On reaching the bottom of Maddocks Hill turn left to follow the roadside pavement in the direction of Crowton and Cuddington. Shortly, over to the left, the Tiger's Head Inn comes into view. On passing the Tiger's Head Inn, enter a narrow path which commences at the side of a tall wooden electricity pole and passes between dwellings. There are modern houses on the right here and the path skirts around their gardens. On the left is the bowling green of the Tiger's Head Inn. Follow the path as it winds and go through a couple of gates. Where the path turns sharply to the right there is a stile at a lower level. Ignore this and follow the path to the right, keeping a fence on the right. Emerge from the fenced-in path at a kissing gate. A well-defined path takes you through trees, and keeps on top of a woody knoll, where there are a couple of vertical footpath signs pointing the way. Pass over a stile at a crossing fence and continue. The path shortly follows the edge of a field where it is fenced in on the immediate right. Where the field finishes, the path continues through trees and undergrowth.

4 A stile at the side of a gate takes you on to a lane, where the way is left. After 50 metres there is a farm on the right. The lane turns to the left now but keep straight ahead through a gap – where there is a footpath sign – and then go over a stile to enter a large field. Cross the field, bearing left, and arrive at a field gate which gives access to a lane. Gradually climb along the lane. At the top of the climb pass three charming dwellings including The Cottage and Wayside. A little further on pass the entrance drive of Westwood and continue past a lane on the left. On meeting a junction of lanes, turn right at the post box to enter Town Farm Lane. Pass the attractive buildings of Town Farm and keep on past The Paddock.

5 Where the lane turns to the left keep forward to enter a facing hedged-in track between The Oranges and a dwelling on the right constructed in 1697. Almost immediately the track forks. Ignore the turning to the right and keep forward shortly to pass by a large modern dwelling which is on the right. Keep forward now to follow a fenced-in track. There are long views to the right across the Weaver valley. The track leads to a facing stile. Cross the stile and walk straight over a crossing track to descend along a path, keeping a wire fence and a wood on your immediate left. At the bottom of the descent cross a stream via a wooden plank-bridge and stile. Climb forward up a grassy bank and cross a dirt-track which is used for vehicle competitions. Climb on and reach a rough, but generally level, field. Continue in the same general direction as before and once again cross the dirt-track to arrive at a stile in a crossing fence. Go over this stile and walk forward across the next field to a stile at the left side of a field gate about 150 metres away. The stile gives access to a lane where the way is left.

6 A straight 150 metres along the lane takes you to crossroads. Turn left now and walk along the grass verge on the right-hand side of the road. Pass Brownmoss Equine Clinic and continue to where, on the right, a sign points along a fenced-in track towards Hatchmere and School Lane. Follow this track which quickly turns to the right. The track takes you to a large field where the way is forward along the field edge, keeping a hedgerow on your immediate right. At the field corner go through a gate. A fenced-in path emerges onto a track close by a dwelling. Keep forward here and, after 250 metres, the track bends to the right. A straight 120 metres takes you to a crossing road close by the Carriers Inn.

The Stanley Arms

THIS WALK IS ENTIRELY WITHIN THE PEAK DISTRICT NATIONAL PARK, WHERE THE EFFORT OF CLIMBING IS REWARDED WITH MAGNIFICENT VIEWS ACROSS MILES OF ROLLING COUNTRYSIDE. THE OUTWARD JOURNEY IS ALONG TRACKS AND INVOLVES A CLIMB TO FOREST CHAPEL. THE RETURN LEG TAKES YOU THROUGH A LUSH VALLEY AND REWARDS YOU WITH VIEWS OF THE POINTED PEAK OF SHUTLINGSLOE.

This hilly district in the east of the county completely contradicts any argument that Cheshire is flat. This walk wanders along the fringes of Macclesfield Forest from where there are long views to Shining Tor, Windgather Rocks, Kerridge Hill and Shutlingsloe.

THE STANLEY ARMS sat, for many years, at the side of the main road to Buxton. Following alterations to the route of the A537, the inn is now located in a rather remote spot with the majority of through traffic passing by to the north. However, this very remoteness is a source of attraction for ramblers and cyclists because there are some lovely views of the surrounding hills from the inn, which was previously a farm belonging to the curiously named hamlet of Bottom-of-the-Oven. Fresh flowers decorate the rooms at all times and during the summer months there is usually a magnificent display of flowers outside. The inn is owned by Marston's, and a good range of beers is on offer, including real ale favourites such as Burton Bitter and Pedigree. Although it is small, the Stanley Arms has built up quite a reputation for its food, be it from the bar, or in the small restaurant. Meals are served every lunchtime and in the evening and a wide choice is available. The inn has a family room, a beer-garden and an outdoor garden area where children are welcome.

✆ 01260 252414

How to get there: The winding A537 links Macclesfield with Buxton. About 5 miles from Macclesfield a secondary road leaves the A537 in a southerly direction, where a sign tells you that Wildboarclough is 3 miles away. Drive along this road and, after ¾ mile, arrive at the Stanley Arms.
Parking: There is a car park at the inn. Alternatively, limited parking is usually available at Forest Chapel.
Length of the walk: 3¾ miles. Map: OS Landranger 118 Stoke-on-Trent and Macclesfield (GR 980724).

THE WALK

1 From the inn, turn right and then left to walk along a road in the direction of Forest Chapel, Wildboarclough and Wincle. Pass Chambers Farm, then turn next right in the direction of Forest Chapel (½ mile). Enter a track on the right now, which begins

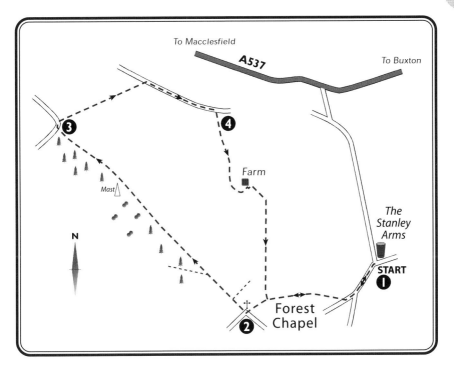

opposite Forest Lodge. The track is stony and climbs quite steeply at first although the going soon becomes much easier. It leads to Forest Chapel, a simple little church erected in 1673 and rebuilt during 1834. The church is well known for its annual Rushbearing Service, held on the first Sunday after 12th August each year.

2 Shortly after passing the church, turn right at the junction and climb the track which runs at the side of Toot Hill House; a sign here says 'Forest Bridleway'. However, before entering this track it is worth walking forward for a few metres to admire long views over Macclesfield Forest. Follow the track as directed, ignoring footpaths which go off to the right and left and keep on past trees on the left. At the top of the climb an electrical reflector mast is set in a clearing on the left.

The views from this spot are excellent. With the mast at your back you can look straight across the valley to the rolling hill of Shining Tor almost 2 miles away. During the summer months hang-gliders and para-gliders are usually to be seen near the summit. To the right of Shining Tor, on the skyline, you will see the Cat and Fiddle Inn which, at over 1,600 ft, is the second highest inn in England. Well to the left of Shining Tor perhaps you can make out the crags of Windgather Rocks, where apprentice rock-climbers learn their trade.

The track descends now, and leads to a T-junction at a crossing lane. Straight ahead, to the right, you should be able to see White Nancy at the far end of Kerridge Hill; there are also long views out across the Cheshire Plain.

3 Turn right; the lane immediately turns to the left, but leave the lane here through a gate on the right. Walk over a short stretch of concrete and quickly pass through a second gate to enter a large rough sloping field. There is a stone wall which descends to your left and another which gradually ascends to your right. Bisect both of these walls by walking diagonally to your left to cross rough open ground. At the field corner go through a gate to emerge at a road. Turn right, and after ¼ mile, leave the road to the right to enter a drive.

4 Cross a cattle grid and continue along the drive. If the day is clear a splendid panorama unfolds ahead towards the pointed peak of Shutlingsloe. Follow the drive as it descends and turns to the left, taking you towards a farm. Pass through a gate about 40 metres before the farm outbuildings and, after a further 20 metres, go over a stile on the right to follow a straight stretch of path between fences close to a large outbuilding. Turn left on reaching the end of this outbuilding, then go over a stile. There is another stile here, in the opposite fence, but do not cross this. Instead, turn right through a gateway and continue, keeping the fence on your immediate left. A hawthorn hedge some 20 metres away on your right runs parallel with the fence on your left.

HALFWAY ROUND THE WALK.

Straight ahead you will see a pair of facing metal gates. Go over a stile to the left of these gates and walk forward for only 10 metres or so, to turn right over a stile. Descend along the edge of a rough field in the direction of Shutlingsloe, which can be seen straight ahead. There is a hawthorn hedge on the right here. At the bottom of the descent cross a stream and stile to ascend along the facing field edge, keeping a fence and stone wall on your immediate right. Go over a couple of stiles at the top of the climb and follow a well-defined path taking you to the left of a farm. Descend steps to arrive at a crossing track close to the church of Forest Chapel which you passed earlier. Turn left and retrace your original route, turn left at the crossing road and then left again to arrive back at the Stanley Arms.

The Three Greyhounds

THIS SHORT WALK AROUND SHAKERLEY MERE NATURE RESERVE IS ONE WHICH WILL GIVE TREMENDOUS PLEASURE TO NATURE LOVERS. ALTHOUGH THE WALK IS SHORT IN TERMS OF DISTANCE, IT IS LONG IN INTEREST. INFORMATION BOARDS PROVIDE A WEALTH OF DETAIL AND YOU WILL ARRIVE BACK AT THE CAR WITH THE IMPRESSION THAT YOUR JOURNEY WAS FAR IN EXCESS OF 1½ MILES.

Shakerley Mere and the surrounding woodland support a diverse range of wildlife and each season presents an ever-changing scene. The woodlands are host to most of the familiar species of birds, whilst Canada geese, mallard, heron, mute swans and black-headed gulls are a common sight on the waters of the mere. Cormorants fly to these waters from their coastal breeding grounds to feed on the fish, and more exotic visitors arrive at different times of the year. Heather thrives in the area and the heathland is of recognised importance and designated as a site of botanical interest. Fishermen can pit their skills against carp, bream, perch and the predatory pike.

In an area where farming is a way of life, it is perhaps not too surprising to learn that **THE THREE GREYHOUNDS** was originally a farm. Its strategic location at the junction of two former drove roads, one between Northwich and Congleton and the other between Knutsford and Middlewich, made an ideal site for an inn where weary travellers could take a break from their journeying to rest and refresh themselves. A familiar feature to these travellers of yesteryear would have been the 250-year-old yew tree that stands in front of the inn. The Three Greyhounds has a spacious and comfortable lounge where a range of Greenalls Whitley beers, draught cider, and cooked lunches are provided. The inn has built up a good reputation for its home-cooked pies. If the weather is favourable, visitors may like to take their refreshment on a picnic table in the grassed area at the side of the inn and where children are welcome. Well-behaved dogs are permitted in the taproom.

Ø 01565 722234

How to get there: The B5081 is used as a link between Middlewich and Knutsford. Close to where the road passes over the M6 there is a staggered junction with the B5082. The Three Greyhounds is situated near this junction on the B5082 road.

Parking: There are generous parking facilities at the pub. Alternatively, car parking is available at Shakerley Mere.

Length of the walk: 1½ miles. Map: OS Landranger 118 Stoke-on-Trent and Macclesfield (GR 730710).

THE WALK

1 On leaving the Three Greyhounds turn left, and then immediately left again, to follow a roadside footpath. After 250 metres arrive at one of the entrances to Shakerley Mere Nature Reserve. There are a number of alternative walks which could be undertaken, although it is probably best to keep to a set configuration.

2 Enter the site and walk forward to arrive close by the edge of the mere. Turn right and follow a well-defined path to shortly pass over a wooden footbridge. The path is never far from the water's edge and there are countless opportunities to observe the wildlife. The mere was formed after large excavations were

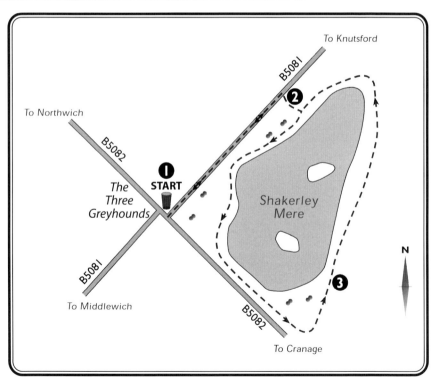

The path around Shakerley Mere never wanders far from the water's edge.

carried out to recover a particular type of sand which was used in the manufacture of coloured glass. The ensuing hole was then filled with water and the surrounding area subsequently landscaped. A number of islands were also constructed.

3 Towards the southerly end of the mere, the path takes you away from the water's edge for a short distance, and then turns to the left to run parallel with the M6. On reaching the head of the mere the path turns to the left and leads back to the entrance gate. Leave the site at this point and retrace your original route back to the Three Greyhounds.

The Swettenham Arms

LIFE JUST AMBLES ALONG HERE AND TO STROLL AMONGST THE GENTLE RIPPLES OF THE SURROUNDING LANDSCAPE IS AN IDEAL WAY TO RELAX. THE OUTWARD PART OF THE WALK TAKES YOU BY KERMINCHAM HALL, WHILST THE RETURN LEG HAS AN ABUNDANCE OF FIELD PATHS AND STILES.

The tiny village of Swettenham sits on the north bank of the river Dane in the heart of rich agricultural land. The village has changed little over many years and rewards the visitor with scenes of pastoral splendour.

THE SWETTENHAM ARMS is tucked away behind the village church. It is a delightful country inn which can boast a long and varied history. Although most of the heavily timbered building that we see today dates from the 16th century, the origins of the inn reach even further back into the past. From as early as the 13th century the site was occupied by a nunnery which, amongst its other functions, catered for funeral parties attending burials at the nearby church. Perhaps these activities were responsible for the eventual change of the site to licensed premises. Visitors to the inn will discover a warm, friendly and informal atmosphere. Imaginatively prepared English cooking is provided at sensible prices and there is a choice of superbly kept real ales, fine wines and malt whiskies. Meals are served every day at lunchtime and in the evenings. The inn has a beer garden and a garden area for children.

✆ 01477 571284

How to get there: Swettenham is situated 2½ miles due east of Holmes Chapel and is about 3 miles by road from Twemlow Green and the A535. The Swettenham Arms is located at the rear of the village church.

Parking: There is a huge car park in front of the Swettenham Arms.

Length of the walk: 3 miles. Map: OS Landranger 118 Stoke-on-Trent and Macclesfield (GR 800672).

THE WALK

1 On leaving the car park, turn left in front of the church where a grassy track takes you to a stile at the side of a gate. Cross the stile and turn right to follow the edge of a field, keeping a fence and trees on your immediate right. Over to the right here is a splendid brick and timber house. A stile at the field corner gives access to a narrow lane. Turn right here and, after only 25 metres, turn left to descend along a rough lane through trees. Cross Midge Brook and climb to a crossing track which is accessed through a gap at the side of a gate. There are dwellings here.

2 Turn left along the track and shortly go through a gate, then a second gate close to a farmhouse, where the track has become a macadam lane. Follow the lane through farm outbuildings. It then turns to the right where Jodrell Bank telescope comes into view straight ahead. On reaching buildings follow the lane as it turns sharply to the left, then bear right, and descend past a pond. Sitting on a rise on the left is the imposing building of Kermincham Hall. Follow the lane for almost ½ mile and emerge on a crossing road. Turn right.

3 Pass Rowley Hall and soon after passing the next dwelling on the right (Rowley Lodge), leave the roadside over a stile to the right. Pass close to a pond and walk forward across a rough field to converge gradually with a wall you will see straight ahead. Go over a stile at the field corner which is set next to this old

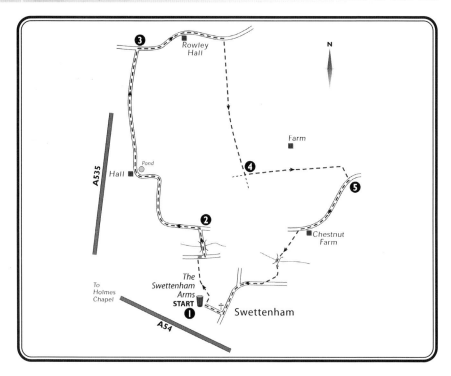

wall, which denotes the old boundary of the land belonging to Kermincham Hall. The path hugs the wall across the next field. Drop down into a hollow at the field corner and cross over a stile. The path gradually leads away from the wall now and takes you to a stile about 150 metres away in a crossing fence. On crossing the stile there is a junction of paths.

4 Turn left here to follow a field edge keeping a fence and hedge on your immediate left. The field edge follows a line of telegraph poles now. Go over a stile at the field corner and continue along the next field edge. Walk straight across a farm approach track to go over a stile which is six paces beyond a telegraph pole and continue along the next field edge. About 80 metres further on go over a double stile on the left and continue in the same general direction as before, but now with a fence and trees on your right. After crossing another stile at the field corner the path has turned to the right, still following a field edge, and leads to a crossing lane via a stile at the side of a gate.

5 Turn right along the lane which takes you past Cross Lane Farm. Follow the lane as it bends to the right (there is a public footpath which goes off to the left here – but ignore this). Keep on past Chestnut Farm, after which the lane has become a track and 120 metres further on arrive at a stile on the left. Go over this stile and descend along a well-worn path. The area is kept as a nature reserve and we are asked to protect the surroundings by avoiding damage or disturbance to plants and other wildlife. Cross a stout wooden footbridge taking you over Midge Brook and keep to the right and climb up a facing embankment to continue across a rough undulating field. Near the top of the climb bear right and walk to a stile which gives access to a lane where the way is right. Follow the lane as it turns to the left near a telephone box. Pass White Rose Cottage and other dwellings then turn right at the church to arrive back at the Swettenham Arms.

The Headless Woman

T HE WALK IS EASY GOING AND, ONCE OUTSIDE THE PERIMETER OF THE VILLAGE, A COMBINATION OF FIELD PATHS AND COUNTRY LANES TAKE YOU THROUGH A PEACEFUL RURAL LOCALITY.

Duddon was once at the very edge of Delamere Forest which in medieval times covered a vast area of the Cheshire countryside. However, the ensuing deforestation has created an area of rolling countryside overlooked and protected by the adjacent Willington hills. This cosy village, with its charming cottages and scattered smallholdings, was once at the centre of a thriving farming community, with the majority of residents working on the farms and living in tied cottages. Although farming is still important, many of the present-day dwellings are owned by people who earn their livings away from the village.

THE HEADLESS WOMAN inn derives its name from the story of a maid who worked at nearby Hockenhull Hall. She was approached by Cromwell's troops during the Civil War and asked to reveal the hiding place of her employer's jewellery. When she refused, the soldiers tortured and then beheaded her. She is still reputed to walk between the inn and Hockenhull Hall, so keep a sharp eye open on this walk! During the 1930s the landlord, a Captain Clayton, placed a figure from the stern of a ship in the garden of the inn. This effigy of a headless woman was a well-known landmark to those passing the inn; unfortunately, it was stolen a number of years ago. The inn's comfortable and cosy lounge has low beams and an abundance of brasses. A range of Greenalls Whitley beers is available as is draught cider. A wide choice of good-value food is on offer and diners have the option of eating bar snacks in the lounge or using a small adjacent restaurant. Meals are served every lunchtime and evening. At the side of the inn there is a beer garden and an amusement area for children. The landlord allows well-behaved dogs in the garden area but not inside the inn.

☎ 01829 781252

How to get there: Duddon straddles the A51 midway between Tarporley and Tarvin. The Headless Woman inn fronts on to this road in the centre of the village.

Parking: There is a large car park at the side of the inn.

Length of the walk: 3½ miles. Map: OS Landranger 117 Chester (GR 512648).

THE WALK

1 On leaving the inn, go through a gap at the corner of the car park and follow a path through the beer garden to emerge onto a lane through a gap in the hedgerow. Turn right and walk along Back Lane. Pass Greenacres and Laurel Park, to arrive at a T-junction, where the way is right. On the left now is the fine black and white building of Duddon Old Hall, which has belonged to the same family for generations. A straight 80 metres takes you to the main road.

2 Turn left here in the direction of Nantwich and follow the roadside footpath. Pass the small brick building of St Peter's church and its adjacent school. After a further 200 metres there is a roadside farm on the left. Turn left immediately on passing the farm to enter a grassy track leading away from the road. This track commences almost opposite a mock black and white farm building on the other side of the road. A straight 80 metres takes you to a field gate. Go over a stile at the side of the gate and walk forward to descend along a large, rough field. Pass to the right of a telegraph pole and go over a footbridge. Climb up the facing field in the same direction as before. The path reaches more level terrain, then takes you to the left of a large isolated tree about 15 metres before the end of the field is reached. Go over a facing stile to enter a large undulating field. Turn diagonally right now

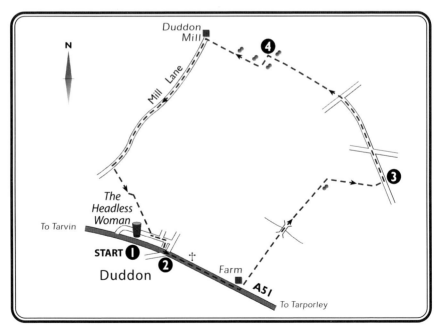

and walk to the field corner, which is about 250 metres away. A stile at the field corner gives access to a short length of track taking you to a lane at the side of Laburnum Cottage.

3 Turn left, pass in front of the cottage, and continue along the lane to a crossroads. Go straight over and walk along the facing Well Lane. Pass The Beeches and Pembroke House to arrive at another crossing road. Walk straight over this and enter a facing hedged-in grassy track. There is an attractive detached modern dwelling on the right here. After 200 metres a stile at the side of a gate gives access to a very large field. Keep forward across the field, bearing right, and walk towards trees which you will see 250 metres away across the field.

4 Go over a combined footbridge and stile at the end of the field and emerge on a track, where the way is left. After 70 metres follow the track as it turns to the right. There is a tall hedge of trees and conifers on the right now, and on the left a rough, sloping field. After a further 250 metres the track takes you on to a lane close by a farm which is on the site of the ancient Duddon Mill, where the waters of the common brook were utilised to turn the old mill wheel. Fruit is now the mainstay crop of the present farm.

Turn left and follow the lane away from the farm. This pleasant lane winds between high-banked hedges. After ½ mile leave the lane to the left, over a stile at the side of a gate. Follow a path along a field edge – keeping a hedgerow on your immediate right. After 80 metres arrive at the field corner. Go over a stile at the field corner close by a gate. Continue, as before, and after 70 metres go over another stile in a crossing fence. Continue in the same general direction as before, keeping a hedgerow on your immediate right. After a further 200 metres pass through a wide gap in a crossing hedge. Bear right and then go over a stile at the side of a gate which is about 30 metres from the field corner. Turn right to follow a lane and arrive back at the path which leads through the beer garden of the Headless Woman inn.

The Red Lion

Although this walk is entirely over level terrain, during the initial stages, when crossing fields, there are views across to the Welsh foothills. The walk does in fact take you over the border, but you stroll in Wales for just one mile before reaching the village of Lower Kinnerton, after which a series of field paths lead back to Dodleston and the Red Lion.

Although Dodleston is only just over 1 mile from the busy A55 along which thousands of summer sun-seekers travel to the coastal resorts of North Wales, it is doubtful if any of these drivers and their passengers are ever aware of this peaceful village where dairy farming is the mainstay of the local community.

THE RED LION inn dates back over 350 years to a time before the beginning of the English Civil War. Records show that an inn existed at Dodleston in 1640 when the Chester to Wrexham road passed through the village. Although this highway has lost its dominance to the nearby A483, the inn we see today provides an excellent range of refreshments for the traveller. The Red Lion has a cosy atmosphere; do not be surprised if you hear some of the customers speaking in Welsh, for the inn is less than a mile from the border. The beers are brewed in Cheshire by Bass and the inn offers a wide choice of tasty food served every lunchtime, and also each evening, except on Sunday. The menus are regularly changed and the inn provides a range of meals especially for children. At the rear, close to the car park, there is a beer garden and an area with amusements for children. The landlord does not permit dogs inside the inn.

✆ 01244 684001

> **How to get there:** The village of Dodleston is 4 miles to the south-west of Chester at the centre of a triangle formed by the Welsh border and the A55 and A483. The Red Lion inn is in the middle of the village.
>
> **Parking:** There is a large car park at the rear of the inn, alternatively there is a car park close to the village church.
>
> **Length of the walk:** 3½ miles. Map: OS Landranger 117 Chester (GR 361611).

THE WALK

① On leaving the inn, turn right and follow the roadside footpath. Turn right shortly in the direction of Pulford and Wrexham, although you may wish to keep straight ahead here to make a short visit to the village church. Dedicated to St Mary, the church is close to the site of Dodleston Castle. On the exterior of the north wall of the church tower are marks said to have been caused by the firing of muskets during the Civil War (1642-49). Follow the roadside footpath in the direction of Pulford and Wrexham. Pass the village hall (1896) to where, shortly after passing Glebe House, the road bends to the left. Leave the road here to the right and pass over a stile at the side of a field gate. Follow a field edge, and, keeping a fence on your immediate right, go over a plank-bridge and stile. Continue, with a hawthorn hedge on the right, and then pass over another stile at the side of a field gate. Turn left now and after 10 metres go through a gap in a crossing fence and proceed along a track, keeping a hedge on the immediate left. Cross a stile, there is a fence and ditch on your left now. At the field corner go over a stile at the side of a gate and almost immediately pass through a gate to enter a large field. Walk forward and gradually converge with a hedgerow on the right and arrive at a field corner. A wooden bridge takes you across a large water-filled dyke. This dyke forms the border between England and Wales and for the next mile you will be walking in the county of Clwyd. On crossing the dyke keep in the same direction as

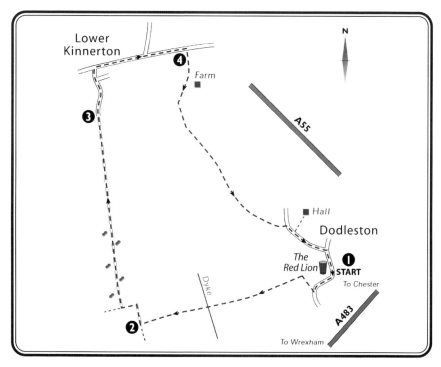

before to follow a field edge where there is a fence and dyke on your immediate right. Straight ahead, the Welsh hills can be seen, with Hope Mountain dominant.

2 A stile at the field corner takes you on to a track where the way is right. Follow this as it shortly turns to the left. After a further 50 metres there is a junction of tracks. Turn right here to walk along a track which is hedged-in by trees on both sides.

3 After ¾ mile the track becomes a lane close by low-lying farm outbuildings. Keep forward along the lane and pass Moor Crescent to arrive at a T-junction in the village of Lower Kinnerton. The way is right here to follow the roadside footpath. Pass a lane which goes to Bretton and Broughton. The roadside footpath finishes shortly, but continue past Warren Wood then, about 150 metres further on, go over a stile on the right at the side of a gate, just before a dwelling on the left is reached.

4 A rough track follows a field edge close to a hedge on the left. Pass through a gap in a hedgerow at the field corner to where, about 80 metres further on your left, there is a crossing place over a dyke immediately followed by a stile which leads you to a large field. Turn right now and walk to a stile some 150 metres away which is about 100 metres to the left of the field corner. Go over the stile, cross a plank-bridge, and follow a path across the edge of the next field to another stile about 120 metres away at the field corner. Go over the stile, cross a plank-bridge, and follow a path going diagonally left across the next field to where a gap at the corner gives access to a large field. The path runs diagonally left and your aiming point is between a farmhouse and a couple of large trees about 250 metres away. On crossing the field a stile at the side of a gate gives access to a lane, where the way is right. Pass the entrance drive of Dodleston Hall and enter the village of Dodleston. On passing the post office turn next right to arrive back at the Red Lion inn.

The Blue Bell

A WALK THROUGH AN AREA OF THE COUNTRYSIDE WHERE AGRICULTURAL PRODUCE IS VERY MUCH TO THE FORE. THE ROUTE IS ALONG NARROW COUNTRY LANES, ACROSS FIELDS AND ALONG TRACKS WHERE YOU CAN OBSERVE AT FIRST HAND AN ALMOST FORGOTTEN WAY OF LIFE IN A VERY SCENIC AREA OF RURAL CHESHIRE.

For the past 200 years Smallwood has provided the Potteries with much of its fresh vegetables. Records show that a number of local farmers had contracts with the great Burslem Co-op and kept numerous horses for pulling their fruit vans about.

THE BLUE BELL is a most attractive little inn, located in a picturesque setting. As with many Cheshire inns the Blue Bell was originally a farm and its origins go back over 300 years. Outside a real blue bell is incorporated into the pub sign, whilst inside there is a wealth of low beams, stone floors and antique high-backed benches forming a small enclosure in the bar. The inn serves a range of Greenall Whitley beers each day at lunchtime and in the evenings (except Monday lunchtime when the inn is closed). Food is served on the same days between 12 noon and 2 pm. When the weather is fine, visitors can take their refreshment in an adjacent garden.

℘ 01477 500262

How to get there: The scattered rural hamlet of Smallwood lies between the A34 and A50 equidistant from Sandbach and Congleton. From the A34 and about 2 miles to the south of Congleton, is Childs Lane. A road sign here points towards Brownlow and Smallwood. The Blue Bell is just over 1 mile along this lane on the right. From the A50 at Fourlanes End a lane goes off towards Smallwood and Congleton. The inn is about 1½ miles along this lane on the left.

Parking: The inn has a car park. Alternatively, there is a parking lay-by at the side of a lane close to Alcumlow Hall Farm just off the A34 about ¾ mile to the north of the entrance to Little Moreton Hall.

Length of the walk: 3½ miles. Map: OS Landranger 118 Stoke-on-Trent and Macclesfield (GR 821607).

THE WALK

1 On leaving the inn turn right and pass The Galleried Barn and Jubilee House Farm to follow a narrow hedged-in lane. Pass Spen Moss Cottage and 30 metres after the entrance drive of Spen Moss Farm fork right to proceed along a grassy track. Just before the track turns sharply to the right at a facing gate go over a stile on the right to enter a large field. With the stile at your back walk forward and pass close to an isolated tree. Pass to the right of another isolated tree to go over a stile in a facing fence. Follow a field edge now keeping a hedgerow and trees on your immediate left. After 200 metres there is a pond among the trees on your left. The field edge turns to the left now but keep forward, bearing slightly right, and pass to the right of an isolated telegraph pole in the middle of the field. On reaching the far side of the field, cross a stile and gradually climb to converge with a hedgerow on the right. Go over a pair of stiles at the field corner; there is a farm about 30 metres to the left of these stiles. Turn left and then right to follow the garden hedge of the farm. Pass over another stile to enter a lane.

2 Turn left and follow the lane past the Methodist chapel which has been converted into a dwelling. A little further on arrive at Lesser Reeves Farm on the left. Leave the lane to the right now to follow a path which commences at the end of a fence. Follow the path along a field edge with a hedgerow on your immediate

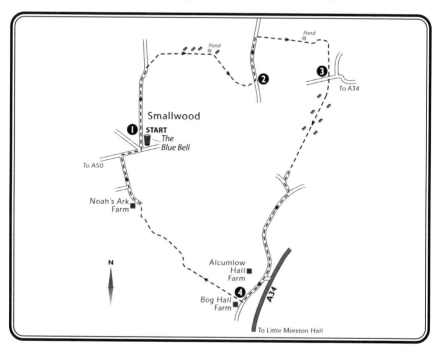

left. On the skyline over to the right can be seen the folly at Mow Cop. Enter a short length of hedged-in grassy track through a gap at the field corner and continue to the next gap in the hedgerow on your left. Go through this and turn right close by a pond then follow a path which hugs the hedgerow on the immediate right as it turns left and right. Join a track and pass between a large low-lying building on the left and other farm buildings on the right. The track turns to the right by another barn. You are now at a junction of ways. Ignore a grassy track which goes off to the left and keep forward along a macadam lane to pass the main entrance drive to the farm on your right. Pass an old dwelling and keep forward along the lane. The way forks shortly where there is a green area on the left. Keep to the right and after 50 metres arrive at a crossing road.

3 Go straight across the road and enter a grassy track hedged in by ferns, brambles and trees. The track becomes a path which eventually emerges close to houses at Brownlow Heath. Turn next left at the crossing lane and then next right by Ivy Cottages to enter Brook Lane. Continue along the lane and after ¼ mile pass a pair of cottages (Alcumlow). After a further 250 metres keep right and follow the lane past the entrance drive of Alcumlow Hall, and continue past Chance Hall Cottage.

4 Turn right just before Bog Hall Farm and leave the lane to enter a straight length of facing track leading through trees. The track becomes a path which emerges into a field through a pair of stone gate pillars. A dwelling can be seen from this point about ¼ mile away across the field. Turn right now to follow a grassy track which turns left along the field edge, then winds around the field edge to join a gravel track at the right hand side of a dwelling. Pass close to the dwelling and then follow a rough lane away from it (Noah's Ark Farm). Pass a farm and continue past a track which goes off to the left. The lane takes you to a crossing road. Turn right and after ¼ mile arrive back at the Blue Bell Inn.

16 HAUGHTON MOSS

The Nag's Head

THIS WALK PROVIDES AN OPPORTUNITY TO EXPLORE THE HISTORIC VILLAGE OF BUNBURY. IT IS A PLEASANT AND VARIED EXCURSION INTO AN INTERESTING AREA OF CHESHIRE, AND FOLLOWS FIELD PATHS, TRACKS AND QUIET COUNTRY LANES.

Bunbury is situated in rich farming country close to the central Cheshire Sandstone Ridge. The village contains many old half-timbered cottages and is dominated by a very beautiful church, the origins of which date back to the 8th century.

THE NAG'S HEAD, dating back to the 17th century, is somewhat off the beaten track, but definitely worth searching out. In its lovely rural setting, it could almost be described as the archetypal Cheshire inn. It is a free house and serves a range of Tetley and Burton ales together with draught Olde English cider. Once discovered, visitors come from far and wide to sample the excellent cuisine, and it is hard to imagine that the attractively decorated dining-room was once a forge where the village blacksmith carried out his trade. Apart from a regularly changing list of 'Chef's Daily Specials', the standard menu offers a wide choice of meals. Except on Mondays, when the inn is closed, food is served every lunchtime and evening. Children may eat in the dining-room away from the bar. When the weather is fine, drinks may be taken in an adjacent beer garden, at the side of which there is a play area for children. When the weather is on the chilly side real fires provide a warming glow.

✆ 01829 260265

How to get there: The A49 bypasses Tarporley and heads due south towards Whitchurch. About 4 miles to the south of Tarporley is the hamlet of Spurstow, where there are crossroads. Drive in an easterly direction from the A49 (towards Haughton) and after 2 miles arrive at the tiny village of Haughton Moss. The Nag's Head is about 400 yards further on.

Parking: The Nag's Head has a large car park. Alternatively, at the centre of the village is a junction of lanes, one of which is called Ferret Oak Lane. To the left of this lane, verge parking is available.

Length of the walk: 5 miles. Map: OS Landranger 117 Chester (GR 580561).

THE WALK

1 From the inn turn right and follow a lane which passes the Coach House. Only 100 metres after leaving the inn go over a stile on the right where a footpath sign points away from the lane. This stile is at the side of a gate and is set close to a

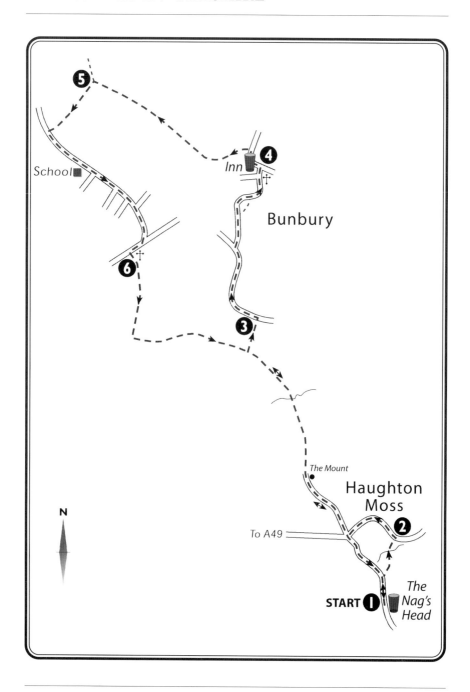

telegraph pole. Bear diagonally left and walk across a field, aiming to the right of houses you will see about 250 metres away through trees. On meeting a facing hedgerow go over a stile about 30 metres from the field corner and enter a rough field. Bear left and, after about 100 metres, go over a sturdy footbridge. Turn right now to follow a narrow fenced-in path which takes you close to a dwelling. Cross a stile and enter a lane.

2 Turn left and pass the houses used as your earlier aiming point and continue along the lane. Pass a dwelling on the right (1895) and a large farm on the left, to arrive at a junction where there is a small green area straight ahead with a couple of seats. Turn right here to enter Ferret Oak Lane (this is the alternative parking area). On passing a dwelling called The Mount, the lane becomes a track between hedgerows and goes past an isolated house. A few metres further on, go over a stile at the side of a field gate to enter a long narrow field. Walk forward along the middle of the field and then descend slightly to the right-hand field corner. Go over a stile and footbridge here and then after a further 40 metres, go over a stile at the side of a holly bush. Follow a well-defined path across the next field which is often planted with maize, a crop which can grow to over 6 ft in height. The field is about 400 metres across. Where the path almost reaches a corner hedgerow which juts out into the field it turns slightly to the left, in the direction of a row of trees which can be seen straight ahead. On reaching the trees, go over a stile and turn right to follow a tree-lined track to a crossing road.

3 Turn left and follow the roadside pavement past dwellings. The road turns to the right and is then much narrower. A little further on, turn right to enter Wyche Road. You are now walking in the general direction of Bunbury church, straight ahead. There is a pond down on the right shortly. A little further on, go over a stile on the right (opposite a dwelling called Wyndhurst) and enter a field. Keeping the garden hedge of a

dwelling on your immediate left, follow the field edge. The dwelling on your left is the Chantry House and dates from 1527. It is of box-framed construction and has recently been restored. Shortly return to Wyche Road via a kissing gate, and turn right to climb up to the church, passing picturesque cottages en route. Visitors are most welcome at the church, which is dedicated to St Boniface who died in AD 755. The church contains the alabaster tomb and effigy of Sir Hugh Calveley, who rendered great service to the Black Prince. Sir Hugh instigated the 14th century remodelling of the church and established it as a collegiate church. In 1940, it was severely damaged by a landmine when its roof, windows and half of one side were blown out. Thankfully, the main structure remained intact and all the damaged areas were restored.

④ On leaving the church, pass in front of the Dysart Arms and turn left to enter College Lane. Pass the National Sunday and Daily School (1830) which is now a private dwelling. A little further on, there is a dwelling on the left. Go over a stile on the right of the entrance drive to the dwelling and at the side of a field gate. Turn left and walk along a field edge with a stone wall on your immediate left at first. Keep to the right of a hedge jutting out from the left to descend along a hollow in the field. At the bottom of this short descent go over a stile set in a fence. Walk forward now across more level terrain where there are trees on the left and then pass over a plank bridge and stile. This bridge is directly beneath overhead power lines. On crossing the stile turn right and follow a well-defined path where there is a fence on the right. Go over a stile in a crossing fence and enter a copse along a well-defined path. Cross a stile and continue through the copse, and emerge over a stile.

⑤ The main footpath goes to the right but keep left now to walk along a field edge, with a hedgerow on your immediate left. Pass under power lines and descend slightly. Continue, passing to the right of a small outbuilding used to store hay. Continue, with a hedgerow and trees on your immediate left and very gradually climb. A little further on, pass through a gate and continue along a track which leads past dwellings and takes you to a crossing road, where the way is left to follow the roadside pavement. Shortly across the road on your right you will see the well-proportioned building of the primary school. This was erected in 1874 on the site of a previous building which had stood here since 1594. Since its inception all those years ago the school has been owned by the Haberdashers' Company. Pass The Highlands, Aldersey Way, The Acreage and Willow Drive. At the next junction bear right in the direction of Haughton. Pass Holly Bank, an attractive black and white cottage, and keep right to pass Swan Court. Turn next left to enter Hurst Close and pass the Methodist church.

6 Keep to the right of a row of bungalows along Hurst Court, and go through a kissing gate on the right which gives access to a field. Bear left and cross the field to go through a kissing gate in a hedgerow. Walk to the next field corner, about 80 metres away, and go through another kissing gate. Walk along the edge of two further fields, with a hedgerow on your immediate left and go through further kissing gates. Turn left now to follow a hedged-in path. Emerge at a facing gate, then keep forward, in the same general direction, and follow a path, via gates, over the ends of three fields. After the third field there is a track going off to the left. Ignore this track and go over a facing stile. You are now back on part of the initial route. Follow the facing path back to Ferret Oak Lane and continue to the crossroads at Haughton. Instead of turning left to retrace your steps, a shorter alternative is to walk down the facing lane, past the war memorial, where a stroll of 400 metres takes you back to the Nag's Head.

The Nag's Head

THIS WALK FIRST TAKES YOU ALONGSIDE THE RIVER DEE AND THEN ALONG TRACKS AND LANES BEFORE RETURNING FOR A CLOSER LOOK AT THE INTERESTING VILLAGE OF FARNDON.

The village of Farndon is, quite literally, a stone's throw from Wales. The majority of its dwellings are perched on a prominence overlooking the river Dee, and a famous medieval bridge links it to its Welsh counterpart, the village of Holt.

THE NAG'S HEAD inn, as its name implies, has had a long association with horses. Its situation close to an important crossing place over the river Dee made it a favourite hostelry in the days when horse-drawn coaches were the predominant means of long-distance travel. During the 1820s the landlord, Charles Wright, did not allow women to enter his inn. Thankfully, times have changed and Mr Wright would be surprised to learn that today the inn is managed by Mrs Locker, who ensures that everything runs very smoothly indeed! A real fire warms the open-plan lounge in cooler weather and brasswork adorns the walls, presenting a welcoming atmosphere. A range of Marston's beers is served including Pedigree real ale. The draught ciders are Strongbow and Woodpecker. The inn is open every lunchtime and evening for meals and the menu is one of infinite variety, being changed almost daily, and with vegetarian options always available. The Nag's Head's situation in the midst of an agricultural area ensures that the produce is always fresh and the inn has quite a reputation for its gammon steaks.

✆ 01829 270261

How to get there: Farndon, which straddles the A534 next to the river Dee, is 8 miles due south of Chester. The Nag's Head fronts on to the A534 in the centre of the village.

Parking: There is a car park at the rear of the Nag's Head. Alternatively, there is a riverside car park (and toilets) close by the bridge which links Farndon with Holt.

Length of the walk: 3 miles. Map: OS Landranger 117 Chester (GR 412546).

THE WALK

1 On leaving the inn, turn right and descend past River Lane to arrive at the bridge connecting Farndon and Holt. A riverside path commences on the right here, on the Farndon side of the river. There must have been a crossing place at this point on the river from early times, for Farndon lies on a Roman road. Probably a ford or ferry was used initially, followed by the construction of a wooden bridge. It is known that work on the present stone bridge began during 1345 and apart from Chester bridge it is the only surviving medieval bridge in Cheshire. During the Civil War (1642-49) there were many skirmishes at the bridge, since the river Dee was the dividing

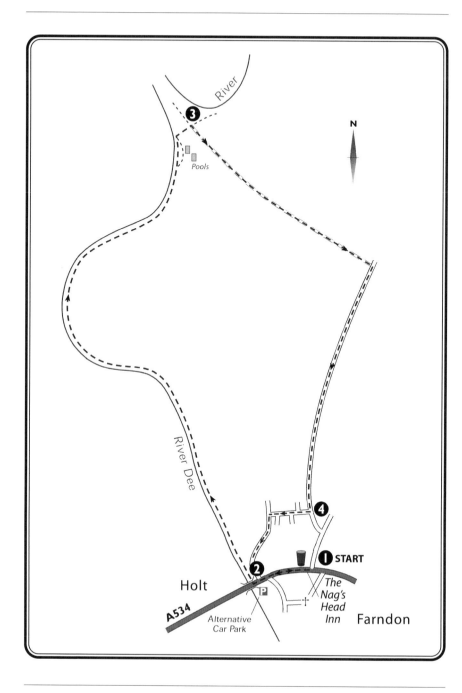

point between parliamentarian Cheshire and royalist North Wales.

2 Follow a well-worn path which never strays far from the riverside and go through a number of gates. There are quite a few weekend dwellings in this area and the path takes you close to many of these. Leaving the weekend retreats behind, the path leads to more open terrain where the fields come down to the water's edge. The river begins to turn to the right; on the opposite bank here can be seen a small footbridge which crosses over a feeder stream. Where the open fields finish go through a gate close to willow trees. A fenced-in path and a rough track take you past an ecological fish farm where a number of man-made pools have been created. The way quickly turns to the left, between a log-cabin and a building covered by corrugated sheeting which has a domed roof, and leads back to the river bank via two gates. Turn right on passing through this second gate and, keeping a fence and trees on your immediate right, walk to a gate which you will see some 80 metres away to the right of a half-hidden dwelling. A kissing gate gives access to a track.

3 There is a footpath straight ahead here, which rejoins the riverside, but ignore this and turn right along the track. After ½ mile, the track turns sharply to the right and becomes a hedged-in lane. A further ½ mile leads to a small estate of bungalows on your right.

4 Turn right here and enter Townfield Avenue. Pass Dee Crescent and Speeds Way (twice) to arrive at a T-junction. Turn left here to enter River Lane, which takes you back to Farndon close to the Nag's Head inn.

It would be a pity to conclude the walk at this point without seeing something more of the village; so if time permits enter Church Lane and stroll past picturesque cottages. Turn next left

THE MEDIEVAL BRIDGE WHICH LINKS ENGLAND AND WALES.

and walk up to the village church, which is dedicated to St Chad. Much of the church was rebuilt following the ravages of the Civil War, at which time an interesting stained-glass window was installed depicting the figures and coats of arms of local families involved in the conflict. Among the memorials in the chapel of the Barnstons is an inscription to Roger Barnston who led his regiment at the relief of Lucknow on 16th November 1857; he is also honoured by a roadside obelisk standing on the northern side of the village. Another well-known son of Farndon was John Speed, who mapped the counties of England during the 16th century; Speed was also an accomplished historian. Leave the church confines along the path leading directly from the porch entrance, then walk along a facing road at the end of which is a rather fine Georgian building. Turn next left to arrive back at the Nag's Head inn.

The Durham Heifer

THIS WALK SKIRTS AROUND THE BASE OF BICKERTON HILL AND
THEN GRADUALLY CLIMBS ACROSS ITS SADDLE WHERE THE
VIEWS CAN BE ABSORBED AT LEISURE. THE RETURN LEG TAKES IN
THE DELIGHTFUL VILLAGE OF BROWN KNOWL WHERE A MIXTURE
OF OLD COTTAGES AND FARMS SIT IN A HOLLOW AMIDST THE EYE-
CATCHING HILL-COUNTRY OF SOUTH-WEST CHESHIRE.

Bickerton Hill presents a fine vantage point, offering outstanding
views across the Peckforton Hills and Cheshire Plain. Its strategic
location was used to advantage by Iron Age man, who built a
fortified stronghold close to the cliffs on its north side.

THE DURHAM HEIFER was once a farmhouse, and this attractive

roadside inn has built up an enviable reputation for its varied and competitively priced food and drink. The Durham Heifer is owned by Banks's Brewery, a company well known for its fine ales, especially its full-bodied and well-hopped bitter. Apart from a good range of beer, draught Strongbow cider is also on tap. When it comes to food the inn can stand comparison with any other hostelry for variety and price. All the food is home-made and hot and cold snacks are always available. Food is served every lunchtime and in the evening. The inn has a beer garden and an adjacent garden area for children. Parties can be catered for by appointment.
✆ 01829 782253

How to get there: Broxton is at the junction of the A41 and A534 some 10 miles to the south-east of Chester. The Durham Heifer inn fronts on to the A534 ½ mile from this junction in the direction of Nantwich.
Parking: The inn has a car park; alternatively, there is a laneside parking area 200 metres along Hill Lane, which leaves the A534 300 metres on the Nantwich side of the inn where a sign indicates that Brown Knowl is ½ mile away.
Length of the walk: 4½ miles. Map: OS Landranger 117 Chester (GR 491543).

THE WALK

1 On leaving the inn turn left, and then left again, to enter a lane where a sign tells you that Duckington is 1½ miles away. After ¼ mile, turn left just before Ivy Farm to enter Ivy Farm Lane. The lane takes you to a crossing lane. Turn right, keep forward past Broomhill Lane, and gradually climb. Turn next left along Sherrington Lane but after only 50 metres turn right to enter Sandy Lane.

2 On passing the entrance to a dwelling called Tanglewood go through a gate, after which the lane becomes a gravel track and

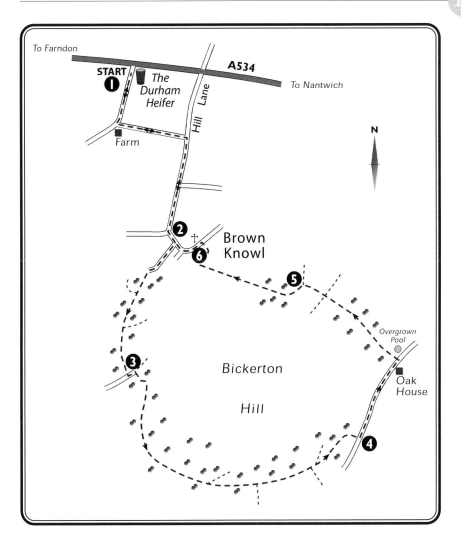

then forks. Keep left here to remain on level terrain and follow a well-defined track through trees. Shortly, there is a junction of ways. A private track goes off to the right, but keep forward to pass through stumps, where a National Trust sign indicates Bickerton Hill. Go through a facing gate and climb between trees and ferns along a sandy path. After about 100 metres you reach level terrain. A track goes off to the left here, but keep forward then descend along a sandy track where a number of telegraph pole-sized supporting logs have been set across the track about 40 metres apart. Pass through a gate and continue along the sandy track. There are pleasant views through the trees on the right now across the Cheshire Plain. Pass close to a small parking area and arrive at a crossing macadam lane through a gate.

3 Turn left here in the direction of the Sandstone Trail. The lane quickly peters out and there is a junction of ways. Turn right here in the direction of Willeymoor and Whitchurch to follow a footpath where the trees form an arch over the path. After about 50 metres, the path kinks to the left up a rough rocky slope and quickly turns to the right. A well-defined track takes you around the base of Bickerton Hill, the bulk of which climbs away to your left. Proceed along the generally level track ignoring any turn-offs which climb up the hill to the left. After about ¾ mile, and shortly after passing a stile on the right, the path forks. Keep forward here and descend where there is an old stone wall on the right. The path leads through a gully and is then walled-in on both sides. Pass through a kissing-gate and arrive at a crossing lane where the way is left.

4 Follow the lane for almost ½ mile and pass some picturesque cottages en route. Shortly after passing Oak House there is an overgrown laneside pool on the left. Turn left just before this pool and follow a sandy track headed by a sign indicating Bickerton Hill. The track skirts the edge of a National Trust car park, leads through a gate, and then gradually climbs through ferns and trees. Ignore a turn-off to the left and 60 metres further on arrive at a junction of ways. Keep forward here in the direction of Brown Knowl but, after only a further 70 metres, turn left where there is another junction of paths. If the day is clear there are long views from this point.

5 Descend here, the path runs across open rock in places and leads, after about 100 metres, to a kissing-gate. Go through this and continue to descend along a path taking you through ferns and trees. Emerge from the trees and enter a sloping field where the village of Brown Knowl can be seen straight ahead. Continue to descend, keeping a fence on your immediate right, in the approximate direction of Brown Knowl church, which sits on a rise straight ahead. On reaching level ground go over a stile at the side of a facing gate and enter a hedged-in track. Follow this as it turns right and then left, pass dwellings and emerge on to a lane opposite Brown Knowl Methodist church.

THE JUNCTION OF PATHS AT
POINT 3 OF THE WALK.

6 Most of the village lies to the right and is well worth a visit although our route is to the left now to gradually climb past Lower Sandy and Sandy Lanes. Turn next right to enter Hill Lane and descend past Broomhill Lane. You are now back on part of your original route. Turn next left into Ivy Farm Lane, turn right again and arrive back at the main road and the Durham Heifer.

The Dusty Miller

Avery simple walk — but one full of interest. From Wrenbury, the route initially follows a lane and then takes you along field paths and over stiles. The return leg is along the towpath of the Llangollen branch of the Shropshire Union Canal, an endless source of fascination with its boats and wildlife.

───────●◆●───────

The stretch of canal passed on this walk, which is the Llangollen branch of the Shropshire Union Canal, was opened at the beginning of the 19th century and radically changed the economy of the neighbourhood. Before the canal was opened all the local produce was transported in rough wagons over poorly maintained roads. The canal made trade much easier with Chester, North Wales, the

Midlands and Manchester. Today, the canal is no longer used for commercial traffic but carries an ever increasing number of holiday craft and provides enjoyment for anglers, bird-watchers and, of course, walkers.

THE DUSTY MILLER enjoys an idyllic location by the waters of the canal, and was formerly a working mill dating back to the 16th century. At the beginning of the 20th century it ceased operating and became a collection point for locally grown produce which would then be taken to various market outlets via the canal. Between the wars the building was used for storing cheese and in its latter days as a storage mill for the then working mill opposite. It became derelict in 1970 and was converted into licensed premises in 1977. Renovation has continued apace since then and the owners can be proud, for their hard work has created a hostelry of great character and charm. Robinson's and Hartleys beers are served, and Strongbow cider is on draught. A wide range of home-made meals is offered at lunchtime and in the evening, and food can be taken in the bar or in the charming 38-seater restaurant on the first floor. There is an extensive canal-side beer garden and a garden area for children.

✆ 01270 780537

How to get there: Wrenbury is midway between Nantwich and Whitchurch and is situated a couple of miles to the west of the A530. The Dusty Miller lies on the north-east side of the village at the side of the Shropshire Union Canal.
Parking: There is a large car park close by the inn and laneside parking nearby.
Length of the walk: 2½ miles. Map: OS Landranger 117 Chester (GR 590480).

THE WALK

1 From the inn, cross the canal over a counter-balanced road bridge. There is a lane which goes off to the left here in the direction of Bickley and Norbury, but ignore this and walk forward along the facing lane. After 150 metres keep forward, ignoring a turn-off to the right, and follow the lane over the infant river Weaver. Pass Porters Hill and follow the lane for a further 400 metres to arrive at a field gate on the left. This field gate is about 20 metres or so before the first large tree on the left is reached.

2 Go over a stile at the side of the gate to enter a large field and walk forward to move very gradually away from the hedgerow on your left. After 150 metres pass under telephone wires and then, 150 metres further on, pass to the right of a low overgrown pond. About 50 metres further on you arrive at the field corner, where a stile in a crossing fence gives access to the next field. Walk straight ahead now in the same general direction as before to follow the line of intermittently planted trees which once formed part of a field edge. After 200 metres go over a stile near a gate and close by an oblong water tank. Cross the next field, in the same direction as before, and go over

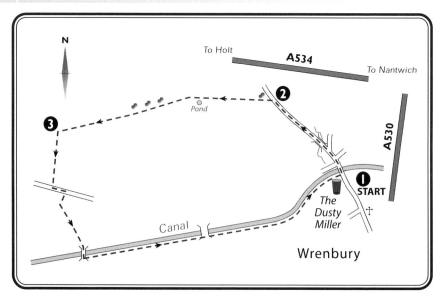

ALONG THE TOWPATH OF THE SHROPSHIRE UNION CANAL,
LLANGOLLEN BRANCH.

another stile set in a crossing fence. Careful navigation is now required. Walk forward in the direction of a telegraph pole which you will see about 150 metres away in the middle of the field.

3 After walking for only about 40 metres, turn left to walk towards the right hand side of a dwelling which is visible about 250 metres away. A stile in a facing hedge to the right of the dwelling gives access to a lane. Turn left and walk along this for about 100 metres then leave the lane to the right over a stile set in a hedgerow. Walk forward and after 40 metres go through a gate to follow a field edge keeping a fence on your immediate right. The path leads to a bridge which takes you over the canal. Now turn right and go over a stile to gain access to the canal towpath. Walk under the bridge you have just crossed (bridge No 22). A gentle stroll of almost 1 mile takes you back to the Dusty Miller.

The Shroppie Fly

T HIS WALK IS FLAT AND EASY GOING, TAKING IN FIELD PATHS, LANES, TRACKS AND A SECTION OF THE SHROPSHIRE UNION CANAL, WHERE THE BOAT PEOPLE CAN BE OBSERVED NEGOTIATING THE SERIES OF LOCKS ON THE APPROACHES TO AUDLEM. IF TIME DOES NOT ALLOW, OR ENERGY IS IN SHORT SUPPLY, THERE IS AN OPPORTUNITY TO HALVE THE DISTANCE OF THE FULL WALK.

Audlem is Cheshire's most southerly town. It is a charming place where the parish church sits atop a high mound overlooking scenes little changed in many long years. The church, dedicated to St James, dates from the 13th century, and contains many items of interest. There is a medieval chest and two old fonts, one of which is said to have been carved before the Reformation. The lofty nave roof is over 400 years old and is carved out of solid oak. The stained-glass windows are fine examples.

THE SHROPPIE FLY stands opposite the 13th lock of the adjacent Shropshire Union Canal, and its origins go back as far as the construction of the canal. It was originally a canalside warehouse which was in use up to 1970. Its unusual name relates to the fact that the bar is partly constructed from a vessel called *The Shroppie Fly*. The 'fly' boats were fast, passenger-carrying vessels, which operated day and night. The pub is a freehouse, hence there is a wide variety of liquid refreshment on offer. Food is available every day from 12 noon to 9 pm. Children have their own menu, and various sandwiches can be purchased. There are tables and benches outside from where all the canal activity can be observed.

✆ 01270 811772

How to get there: Audlem is 6 miles due south of Nantwich at the junction of the A525 and A529. The Shroppie Fly is on the west side of the town by the Shropshire Union Canal.

Parking: The Shroppie Fly has a car park. Alternatively, there are usually one or two parking places available in and around the town.

Length of the walk: 5½ miles. Map: OS Landranger 118 Stoke-on-Trent and Macclesfield (GR 659435).

THE WALK

1 On leaving the inn, turn left and walk up to the Bridge Inn where the way is left. Pass the Methodist church and continue up to the parish church, which sits on a mound overlooking the town. After leaving the church, enter Vicarage Lane, which commences opposite the church entrance steps, and gradually descend. The lane turns to the left shortly – where there is a green area on the right. Leave the lane here, cross the green,

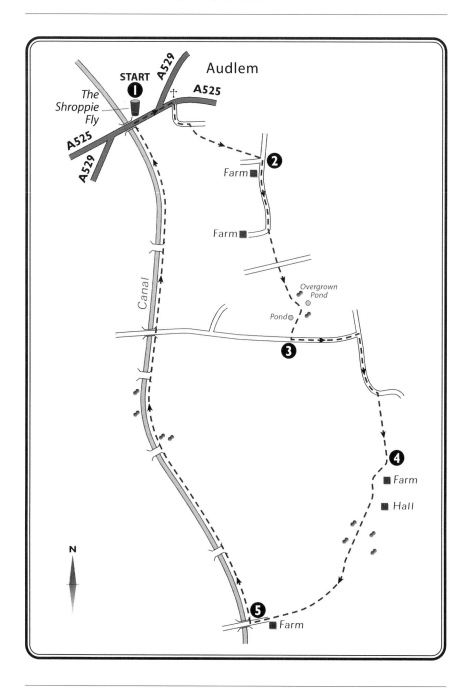

and go over a facing footbridge. There is a stile on the immediate right here but ignore this and go over two facing stiles to enter a large undulating field. Gradually climb along the left-hand edge of the field keeping a hedgerow on your immediate left. Where the hedgerow on the left turns away to the left continue forward in the same general direction to cross the field. Look back here for a splendid view of Audlem, with the church dominating the scene. Continue to the facing field corner and cross a stile.

2 There is a lane going off sharply to the right here, but ignore this and keep forward along a hedged-in lane taking you in the direction of a farm about 100 metres away. Follow the lane and pass the farm. The lane goes across open fields, then shortly turns sharply to the right and leads to Fields Farm, but keep straight ahead here to follow a facing gravel and grassy track, which emerges on a lane at the side of a cottage. Walk straight across the lane and go over a facing stile. Follow a field edge, keeping a hedgerow on your right, but after 50 metres keep forward as the hedgerow on your right gradually turns away to the right. Cross an undulating stretch of field to converge gradually with a fence on the left and then cross a stile at the field corner. Follow the left-hand edge of the next field to turn right by an overgrown pond. In a few metres converge with a hedgerow on the left at a point where there are overhead telephone wires. Go over a stile here and then turn right to pass to the left of a pond where there are rushes. After a further 50 metres go over a stile in a hawthorn hedge. Keep forward, there is a fence on the right now, and after a further 50 metres go over another stile to enter a lane.

3 *If you wish to complete the shortened version of the walk* turn right along the lane, keep forward past Wood Orchard Lane, and in ½ mile arrive at the towpath of the Shropshire Union Canal via a gate at the side of bridge 76. Walk under the bridge and follow the canal towpath into Audlem. *For the full walk,* turn left along the lane. Pass a row of cottages and continue to a junction, and turn right in the direction of Norton-in-Hales. After ¼ mile arrive at a track on the right which goes to Highfields Farm. This track commences at the side of an attractive black and white dwelling. Go over a cattle grid and follow a straight stretch of gravel track in the direction of the farm.

4 About 80 metres before reaching the farm outbuildings, fork right and follow a gravel and grassy track across open land. Go through a gate. After a further 60 metres the track turns to the left and goes towards buildings, but ignore this and keep forward along a grassy track. A few metres further on there is a splendid view over to the left of the half-timbered building of Highfields Hall. The grassy track peters out shortly but keep forward in the same general direction as before to follow a line of large, interspersed, trees. Go through a gate in a crossing hedgerow and continue along a well-defined track which becomes a concrete drive. (You have now entered the county of Shropshire in which you will stay for the next 1½ miles.) Shortly, the drive becomes hedged in and leads towards a large farm. Pass between the farm outbuildings and continue past the farmhouse. A hedged-in macadam lane takes you away from the farm and to a bridge which crosses the Shropshire Union Canal.

5 Do not cross here but go through a small gate on the right and descend to join the canal towpath. Turn right and follow the towpath away from the bridge. After ¼ mile pass under bridge 73. The next 2 miles of the walk is along the canal towpath during which you will pass under bridges 74 to 78. This section of the canal has no less than 12 locks which the boat people have to pass through. On passing under bridge 78, the Shroppie Fly comes into view. A few more strides take you back to the inn.